IN PRAISE OF CHAOS

for Anita —

Trust your

Chaos!

In Praise of
CHAOS

Sean Caulfield

PAULIST PRESS
New York/Ramsey

Library of Congress
Catalog Card Number: 81-82335

ISBN: 0-8091-2396-7

Published by Paulist Press
545 Island Road, Ramsey, N.J. 07446

Printed and bound in the
United States of America

CONTENTS

for
Kristin

"This discord in the pact of things,
this endless war 'twixt truth and truth."

Boethius: *De Consolatione Philosophiae,* V: 13

INTRODUCTION

I have written a book in praise of the splendid chaos of life, the chaos that saves us from the fate of clones and robots and opens our way to incredible futures. Chaos is important. Too often the word is used in a negative sense, as if chaos were something which should not exist. But chaos is the power and wisdom and freedom of God in our midst. We need it.

By the word "chaos" I mean all those random, haphazard happenings, the unpredictable situations in life, the random chances, the rotten luck, the fortuitous events, the uncertainties, coincidences and confusion, the unforeseeable and the uncontrollable. They are the very stuff-of-life that complement the routine expectations of law and order. When chaos occurs people expend their energy in desperate attempts at restoring order. Even Church and state do it. We want to have things in control. This at least is a partial mistake. Out of the chaos comes something new and creative, something not planned at all that order and routine could never have delivered. If we are trapped in order, if we have imposed order on ourselves—and therefore inevitably on others—we have choked off life and growth. Control we may have, and a false security for a time, but change will find us out. Chaos will not be denied.

Chaos offers the possibility of a choice. It is an expression of the world's freedom-to-be. It should be celebrated, reveled in, and embraced. Our energy should be directed toward discovering the new creative possibility that might emerge from it if we choose well.

Chaos, then, is something positive. It is not evil, such as the moral evil of sin. Evil is opposed to order and destroys it. Chaos complements order. So we fall down stairs, break a leg, miss a plane, crash the car; we are late for appointments, find the right book, spill our coffee, lose our wallet; we make friends and enemies, get good and bad advice; we are misunderstood, praised and condemned for the same accomplishment; we experience the death of a loved one and all the horrors and joys that engage us. They are not sin, nor always resulting from sin. They are the chaos of life, a chaos found in social as well as private affairs.

I have a secret feeling that the chaos is more important, in the long run, than the laws and the order. It prevents us from becoming "mass man," the faceless acceptors of totalitarian rule. Those who enforce law and order do so always within a temptation—the unquestioning assumption that power enlightens them on what the "right" thing is that people should be doing, and what the "norm" is for the sort of people we are supposed to be. But we are not machines. Chaos holds out the possibility that we may become people unimaginably greater than anything others could have planned or we anticipated. The unique personality into which we are growing cannot be planned. There is no norm for it. We cannot be legislated into Christian and mature personhood. Only free choices and the decisions of love will bring us to transcendent personhood. Chaos is the place where many of those choices and decisions are made. Law and order are, of course, necessary, but chaos extends us beyond that necessity to a greater fulfillment.

The structure of this book is very simple. The first two chapters attempt to establish a foundation for the validity of chaos as an integral part of our world. The following chapters take a look at key aspects of our experience of living: our moral, personal and social lives; our presence in the world as artists (the people who do good things well); our acceptance of life's chaos as revealed in our praying through the paradoxes of life; the chaos revealed in the history of the spiritual life; the chaos in confronting dying and death. The chapters explore the element of chaos in all of these and try to show that out of the chaos comes growth, change and maturity.

The book is written for all who experience chaos in their lives. It is especially for all the "little ones," the people who are made to feel guilty or who have a poor self-image, thinking that somehow their lives are less worthy because of their confusion. It is a call to relax, to redirect thinking and energy, to revel in the divine providence that underlies life, to discover that all the jumble of events in the past had a purpose after all. For those who have been hurt by the chaos, the victims of power and the institutions, there is a question: "Have you not, perhaps, been challenged beyond yourself to something vastly more wonderful than you have considered?" In a word, this book celebrates human freedom within our incredible chaos.

"In the Beginning"
THERE WAS CHAOS

I have been sitting here at the typewriter for days, staring at a blank page. I don't know how to get started. Really, I don't want to get started—it is part of the chaos. I want to write about chaos, but to write about anything demands that it be done in an orderly fashion. To write about chaos in an orderly fashion seems to be a contradiction, a sort of paradox, at any rate a betrayal. So I sit and stare at the page and my eyes get sore. I remove my glasses, rub my eyes, get up and stretch and decide to make a pot of tea—always a good excuse to avoid something unpleasant. As the tea is being brewed, loose leaves in a coffee pot, I pace up and down thinking of chaos. I have a sort of intuition of chaos, like seeing all the pieces of a jigsaw puzzle suddenly come together to form a unified whole. I feel that I grasp it and I say to myself that if I see it—which is both more and less than understanding it—I do not have to write about it. I walk into a cloud of steam ... "Hang it," the tea is boiling over—it is part of the chaos. Tea should never be boiled; law and order say so. I strain the leaves out, add three spoons of sugar and one of creamer to the mug and taste ... ah-h-h-h! Despite the fact that it still tastes and looks like paint (burnt sienna to be exact), it is the elixir of life. It is rather a pity to reduce one's intuition of chaos to orderly statements. Human order will diminish it. Only divine order is vast enough and wise enough to encompass the chaos in human affairs, see the whole picture clearly and understand it.

Much of our energy is expended in trying to restore order,

trying to get back to normalcy and routine, even to automatic functioning. Quite often it is a waste of valuable energy. The inability of getting back to order leaves us frustrated, exhausted, a bundle of contradictions, with frayed nerves, confrontations, judgmental attitudes and even a sense of guilt. We feel that our security lies in having things go in an orderly fashion, yet we find ourselves confronted with the fact that order is constantly breaking down. Worse still, if we pause to reflect on it, we realize that, like it or not, chaos is here to stay. More than that, it is supposed to be here. It was meant to be. It is an integral part of our world. For people whose lives depend on law and order, chaos is a nemesis. Their energy is all used up in maintaining the order. But some, at least, of the energy should be used to discover the unpredictably new and creative thing that can emerge out of the chaos.

One is tempted to begin at the beginning and say that somebody broke hydrogen and there was a "Big Bang"; somebody made a great ball of fire out of nothing. That is a scientific approach with a philosophical sting to it—"out of nothing." But the Bible does not have anything whatever to say about the science of origins, nor could its writers have even raised the philosophical question. In the matter of creation the Bible answers to the question "Why?" It has no response to the question "How?" Science deals with the "how" of the development of the universe once it is there; it has no answer whatever to the question "Why?" Scripture says: "In the beginning God created the heavens and the earth. Now the earth was a "tohu wobohu" (a formless void, a chaos), there was darkness over the deep, and God's Spirit hovered over the water" (Gen. 1:1). The Genesis account is a rejection of the Mesopotamian and Canaanite myths of creation in which the creative deity had to struggle with an already existing monster, Chaos. The point being made is that God does not have to overcome chaos. Chaos is not an ultimate principle of the origin of things, a creative deity which God had to overcome, and which he never quite vanquished in that it keeps returning in the cycle of the seasons. Genesis denies any dualism of this kind. Creation, as the Bible sees it, is not the victory of a creative deity over a monster. God does not have to struggle at all. Creation is fashioned by God's spoken word and not by effort of any kind. There is no question of his entire supremacy. He commands, and no resistance is made; there is no obstacle to his will. What chaos there is and that exists from the beginning is a valid element of his creation.

The presence of chaos in the world bothers people. They wonder how God could have created an imperfect world. Looking back over the chaos in nature and history down through the centuries they feel that something went wrong somewhere. One of the answers is that he made a perfect paradise on earth but that we destroyed it by sin. The original perfect state was then taken away as punishment. There is truth in this in that Genesis points out that we, and we alone, are responsible for sin. God is not responsible for it. And, yes, sin brings disorder and destructiveness upon the earth. But chaos is not sin nor always the residue of sin. And we know that there never was a paradise on earth in the sense of a static, robot-like, world on which God had imposed perfect law and order. The world he made was not a fully finished paradise. Such a paradise would have been a puppet or a toy. Rather, he made a world destined for freedom, a world-to-be-free, and with the calm maturity of an absolutely secure God he realized quite well how ludicrous the results would be for time as the world struggled toward that final freedom.

What God made was "a world coming into being" (Schoonenberg). It is not his toy. It is its own world, bringing about within itself through chaos and chance, trial and error, cause and effect, what it is capable of becoming. And it is God's creature precisely in doing that. But God does not stand aside. He creates as the intimately-present transcendent ground of the world's development. He did not bring forth a fully finished world but a perfect child. And as in the growing up of every child, his world's future would involve itself in very much chaos. His creative presence to the world is much like that of a mother to her child. Just as a mother cannot spare her child the pains of growth but is present to it in health and sickness, sleeping and walking, laughter and tears, offering her help and love—in fact, all the child needs to grow and be mature—so is God, but with greater intimacy, present to his world. He did not impose adulthood on it. To have done so would have been to stunt its development. The creative act of God does not at all deny or bypass that activity of each of his creatures that is proper to that creature. In fact, it brings it about. God enables all things to be freely what they are capable of being. Each reaches out to be fully itself, and in that collective outreach lies all the chaos. If God imposed anything at all, it was freedom. For example, God made us humans to be free. So God empowers each one of us to choose and decide freely for ourselves to be ourselves. And it is in so choosing that we are most his creatures, children of a creative God. His law and order are not imposed on us as a static perfection. Were that the case we would be clones or robots. It is when we act feeely, with "the freedom of the children of God," that we reveal ourselves as being his handiwork. Now it is this freedom which is the basis of all our chaos. But it is the most precious gift that God has given us. Chaos is that aspect of this world of ours which mirrors back to God his own essential freedom. To him it is no chaos because he sees the entire picture.

Creation is a spontaneous act which can have no other source than an explosive act of love on the part of God. This act of love is the only "Big Bang" that theology can know. It results in an ongoing dynamic universe, a free universe. God did not preset or presuppose anything other than the world's final purpose, union with himself. Love does not presuppose. He loved and that love was freedom, the freedom of the universe to be anything it might possibly be with no limitations placed on its development. The more free the world would become the more would it image the God who fashioned it. Freedom was the greatest gift he gave it. But we with our limited view of things, we who can never see anything from every point of view at one and the same time, experience that freedom as chaos. God has the whole view, seeing the end in the beginning, and not ignoring the world but bringing it to fulfillment. For example: when a man plants wheat he does not do so for the mere sake of planting, nor does he abandon it to its own devices, but he irrigates the field, dusts the crop and cares for it in spite of drought, weeds and pests. The end—bread on the table—is contained in the purpose of what he does. The end is contained in the beginning and endures throughout the entire time it takes for the crop to come to fulfillment. This is even more true of God's creative act. He made a world with a purpose. He is always present to it. But it must develop of itself. For this reason he has placed within it all it needs to achieve that purpose. To speak of the beginning is to speak of the end. It would freely come back to him. It would bear fruit as it has done in Jesus of Nazareth, the first-fruits of salvation. The point is that the creative act of God stretches across the whole of the history of the universe from beginning to end. He never abandoned his emerging world. Because it is still a "world coming into being" it seems to us to be imperfect and chaotic, but the sustaining and guiding providence of God underlies all the chaos, giving the chaos purpose. For God to create is, in effect, to be personally present at the inmost core of reality as its origin, purpose and final transformation. He is the personal savior at whose initiative all comes into existence. He is the source of its free development. As source, presence, providence and transforming power he sees the relevance of its freedom where we see only the chaos.

God made each one of us "in his own image and likeness." That implies freedom, responsibility, maturity and being our own person. God is the source of our becoming who we are destined to be. This destiny is not imposed but must be achieved. The more free we become with ourselves, and the more human, unique and mature we become, the more created we reveal ourselves to be. It is our inner freedom which reveals that we are in his image made. And it is within our chaos that we make the choices and decisions of freedom. There is no need then to fear what seems to us to be chaotic. It is the freedom-to-develop which God has put at the center of all things— "this endless war 'twixt truth and truth." In a finite world of time and space, of change and development, of growing and becoming the freedoms clash and we have chaos—glorious, magnificent chaos in which unthought-of possibilities come to be.

When God's creation reached perfection in Jesus of Nazareth we find that the chaos was only compounded. Before his time the old law spelled things out as "right or wrong." Jesus fulfilled all of this and went on to transcend it. He was himself the Spirit of freedom and he gave us that very same Spirit which transfigures our daily chaos without removing it, and opens us out beyond the narrow boundaries of law. He recreated the situation in which we live, so that from within it we are able to make the choice which leads to the ultimate purpose of creation, union with God. But the offer was made to a sinful world and the outcome for himself was utter chaos. His life, rejection, betrayal and death were absolutely chaotic. He was no robot God-man. His life, for all its sinlessness, was not one of unruffled law and order. It was love within unpredictable chaos.

There were elements there of pure chance, rotten luck, misunderstanding, the unforeseeable and unpremeditated. These were the ingredients of his life within which he chose freely to grow, to be fully human and divine in a response of love to his Father. He called us to the same freedom, to break out of our self-serving interests in deeds of love for others. We crucified him because we could not accept his word or work. Rather than transcend ourselves in free choice we preferred a false security in a law and order society in which we and not God were in control. We are fearful of the chaos because of the price we must pay for our growth. We fear the vulnerability of love within which humans become what they are capable of becoming. We establish a world of order enclosed on itself. We build walls about ourselves. We curse the chaos which keeps tearing down the walls, distrupting the order, challenging the laws.

Christ came to reveal the end that was contained in the beginning of creation. If there is any one thing he taught us, it is that there is no longer a justification for despair or fear in the face of chaos. The end is God, life, resurrection and union. He did not abolish the chaos or restore any impregnable system of law and order. What he did was offer us the possibility of being a new creation in the midst of chaos. In the face of sin, fear and selfishness, and in the reality of confusion and chaos, he expressed again God's creative and explosive act of love. Creation became a new creation. Freedom became a new freedom. As the free children of God he raised us up to an altogether higher level of human existence, a level to which we could not have aspired by human powers alone. Graced with his own life and Spirit, recreated anew in God's freedom, absolved from a legalistic approach to life and God, we have been restored to the original chaos. He has offered us unheard-of possibilities. The creative providence of God has moved one more step closer to us in the abiding presence of his Spirit. It enables us to say "yes" to God. Christ has given us the Spirit which sets us free within the fertile ground of chaos to become people we never imagined we could become, and to reach a destiny that transcends us.

This may threaten people of power who wish to organize life, or people who feel that others are too weak or inclined to evil to be trusted. Chaos has no place in politics, civil or ecclesiastical. But we cannot batten down the hatches and ride out the storm of chaos as immobile cargo in the bark of Peter. To impose perfect order, to eliminate chaos, would be to end the dynamism of growth. It would be a tyranny that destroyed God's creative work itself. For when God saw the end in the beginning he saw that chaos was a sort of sacrament: the visible sign of the invisible reality of God's freedom at the core of our existence. He saw it all and it was very good.

CHAOS IN A PHYSICAL
AND CONSCIOUS WORLD

Isaac Newton was a religious man. His physics could accurately predict the course of certain macroscopic events: "If these sets of circumstances exist now, we can conclude that this other event will certainly take place." He saw this natural law and order as the reflection in the created world of the perfection of God. It gave us dignity. But it somehow suggested that law and order were the only ways in which the perfection of God could be revealed. In the end it suggested a sort of determinism in which we were all helpless parts of a machine whose functioning was fixed and predetermined from the first day of creation.

We are now in an age of quantum mechanics. We have discovered that this world of matter, for all its apparent solidity, is only congealed energy. And Newtonian physics does not apply at the sub-atomic level. Quantum mechanics cannot predict specific events. It deals in probabilities. At the sub-atomic level there is nothing that will "certainly take place." Particles have a tendency to randomness. Nature presents us with variables and law and logic fail us. We are left with choices. The world is not a machine. It is still "coming into being" with a certain freedom-to-develop both at its inmost depths and in the outermost reaches of space.

Everything in the universe, from the Big Bang to the present, is God's creature specifically in its hungering to be more than it is, in its stretching out for a greater grasp on being. From random sub-atomic particles to out-rushing galaxies each created thing, each

12

aspect of reality, reaches out, almost desperately, for a greater measure of being. It is the dynamism of the entire world to hunger for the Absolute. "The whole of creation is groaning as it awaits its deliverance," said St. Paul. To the person of faith, even the conservation of energy in the universe reveals, at its most radical depths, the providence of the Creator compelling all things to survive, to develop and reach beyond themselves to a higher level of being. This reaching has come up from the organization of atoms to molecules and cells, to life and consciousness. It has come to personhood, to touch God in Jesus. This physical body-person, Jesus, can now say: "He who sees me sees the Father." And we who have come out of the clay of the earth can now say: "Abba, Father." Thus far has the clay come hungering for God. Change, growth and becoming are the measure of life in the world.

God placed within the universe everything it needed for its development. But it was free and had to do its own developing, and that is where the chaos, the chance and the unpredictable entered. Let us take, by way of example, this infinitesimally small part of our universe, planet earth. We should realize that life on this planet is sheer good fortune, an event that did not have to be. The chances of this hunk of matter developing life forms, the sheer improbability of the coming together of all the required circumstances which in harmony with one another had the power (from God's creative act) to bring about life here, must have been millions to one. That it developed here is marvelous good fortune for us. But if life had not developed on planet earth, God's purpose would not have been frustrated. It would have happened elsewhere. Astronomers assure us that undoubtedly it has happened many times in the galaxies about us. They, too, contain all the basic building blocks of life. The belief that we are the only life in the universe is megalomanic. We need this reminder of our utter contingency, that we did not have to be, that we do not have to be, that the destruction of life on planet earth would be of no more significance for the universe as a whole than the death of one man is for our world as a whole. This enables us to keep things in perspective. We are not needed. Life here is pure gift, joyful good fortune, while it unfolds as it must within the providence of a loving God. It is a marvelous example of the fulfillment of the freedom-to-be that exists in God's creation. Nothing was imposed, but anything might have evolved freely within the possibilities of the world he made. It is out of a like chaos of possibilities that our own personal existence took place. The incalculable circumstances that brought our forebears together, the act of generation in which any one of two hundred million sperm might have fertilized the ovum rather than the only one whch could have resulted in ourselves, is, from our frame of reference, chaotic. From God's point of view it is love. In the beginning there was only love, and within that love there was freedom-to-be. When it resulted in our being, God saw that it was good.

There were no blueprints. Love does not have blueprints. God did not have a master-plan up his sleeve. It would have destroyed the free creativity of love. The universe was thrown out there with unheard-of possibilities within it, and behold there is life on planet earth, his presence enabling it to develop within chaos, chance and choice. Atoms, molecules and cells worked feverishly. Despite billions of failures there were some successes. Life grew. Trees and crops pushed up out of the earth. Consciousness developed because the possibility of consciousness was there. Everything strove through selection, camouflage and reproduction to have life and have it in greater abundance. The Word of life "through whom, in whom and for whom" all things were made had called them to himself and they were responding.

During the millenniums in which life was developing on the earth, progress was not orderly or automatic. There was considerable chaos. Chance often determined which species survived and which became extinct. A species well adapted to a prevailing climate, living in harmony with its environment, could easily be wiped out when the climate changed. Or in the resulting chaos it would slowly and painfully change and adapt. Oftentimes it was the freaks which survived. An element, freakish in the previous condition, suited the new environment very well. A long neck would enable an animal to eat from the higher branches when drought had destroyed all vegetation at the lower levels. (Need anything be said about the need to stick one's neck out when a change of climate takes place in the Church?) Survival of the fittest has often been the survival of the freaks. Survival has been chaotic. The strange fact is that a freakish element in the past was often beneficial for the future life on our planet. The trouble with the dinosaurs was that they were overspecialized. When they got stuck in the mud they stayed there. They are

14

still with us, of course, as fossils. It is a parable of sorts for us: elements in our world and Church which worked very well in the past, and which for reasons of fear or security have been brought into a different climate, remain with us as cold and dead fossils. Furthermore, what now appears freakish, random, chaotic or unimaginable in our lives, or the life of the Church, may very well be the element which will be beneficial for our future.

One species of life, fortunately for us the "human," developed to where consciousness doubled back upon itself and became self-conscious. We began to reflect upon ourselves and be intelligent. This also was the result of God's creative act, so that ultimately it was he who "breathed into us the breath of life." The circumstances were happily correct; the lobes of the brain had developed. Yet, in this freedom world of ours, thousands of things could have gone wrong which might have prevented it. If the right mammoth lizard had eaten the right prehistoric humanoid at the right time, you might very well be eating this book right now instead of reading it. That is a bit chaotic but you know what I mean. We are utterly contingent, so let's be humble about it. Self-consciousness could affirm or deny, accept or reject, love unselfishly or be possessive, risk further development or be protective and stunted. It was the first conscious test of our freedom. But by reflection we had come to recognize the chaos. The chaos of conflicting options burst on our self-conscious world. It revealed risk and death. We failed the test. Instead of continuing to reach beyond ourselves we opted for ourselves. We chose to protect ourselves against others and, therefore, against further major development. We closed up on ourselves and lost our freedom. Thus sin—humans-enclosed-upon-themselves—entered the world. Perhaps in that primitive state we could not have done otherwise. Perhaps the fault was truly a "happy fault"—the *felix culpa* of the Easter Vigil liturgy. Perhaps we ourselves are still primitive in deep areas of our instincts and feelings. In our progress we were supposed to come to other-consciousness, to the awareness of the rights of others, to reach out in love and justice to them and so transcend ourselves by reaching beyond ourselves. But too much self-consciousness became our destruction, and we devoted our energy to maintaining the status quo, protecting ourselves against the chaos and the challenge to develop. And we brought sin into the world by professing that we were all that was, that a world closed in on itself and sufficient to itself was all that existed. It was, and is, blasphemy. That calm cold assumption of self-sufficiency is the greater sin that underlies all the malicious violence we use to support it. We put our trust in power, wealth and knowledge, in tanks and bombs. It is our choice. The least we might do is not cry about where it has brought us.

We needed Christ to break the chain of evil that bound our world, to set us free into the world of God, to get us moving upward again. He, "the beginning and the end, the Alpha and the Omega," gave us his own Spirit which enables us to reach beyond ourselves. Our chaos is no problem to Christ. It is in the midst of chaos that we, now a new creation in Christ, are able with pain but sureness to make choices. In the free decisions of love we are the designers of our own destiny. In those free choices we are revealed as his creatures, the people of the Spirit.

Sin, which is selfishness, the refusal to acknowledge dependence on God and to accept responsibility for further development toward him, is not correct. It should not exist. But chaos is correct, offering us the possibility of free choice and growth. Law and order are also correct. But chaos and law and order cannot be reconciled. One of them cannot be accepted to the rejection of the other. It is a dialectical situation, a give-and-take tightrope act. What it involves is not necessarily conflict but encounter and dialogue, discernment with flexibility. Order will always challenge chaos as the possible locus of destructive and disruptive forces. Chaos must challenge the instinct of law to impose itself as our only directive. Such an imposition would be tyranny, civil or ecclesiastical. It would kill the creative spirit. The problem is not going to be solved, but out of the encounter will come a new truth, a better course of action if both sides are humble, flexible and wise. In the Church, for example, there is the genuine gift to preserve the tradition. But there is a further prophetic gift which reads the signs of the times so that "like a wise householder" the Church continuously brings forth from its treasury not only old things but new as well. The emergence of the new, the better adapted, may seem freakish at first and create chaos. But the Spirit who is not subject to anyone's laws and "blows where he wills" gives the prophetic gift, moves people to initiate and promote new ways of understanding and proclaiming the message of Christ, new ways of serving God's people, new forms of old devotions. Chaos or not, the Spirit will inevitably be heard and obeyed. We in our stumbling way follow along, and our development remains partial. But the solution is not in more law and order, more right and wrong, but in a new consciousness of the Spirit in our midst. Denouncing wrongdoing is too simplistic a solution. One does not have to be a prelate to do that. What most we want of Church leaders is that they uncover the salvation that is already ours within the chaos, let loose within us the mystical life of the Trinity, of grace and creativity, tell us of the beauty of God and that he is really with us. We want them, further, to revel in the chaos brought about in the demands of culture in Africa, of women in the United States, of liberation in South America. We want them to see that it is evidence of life. We want them to dream of the possibilities for the future that are offered in the choices of today. "Why did you doubt, O you of little faith?" was the question put by Christ to his apostles. The chaos is the only valid sign we have of a God creating a world in freedom. We should shout it from the housetops: "Something new is happening."

How seldom it turns out that way. We are fearful of new things, of the risk in the choices. Recall our myth of Beauty and the Beast. The myth expresses our deeper understanding: that when Beauty kisses the Beast, the Beast is tamed and converted. We do not risk that. We send out the National Guard or whatever powers we possess to kill King Kong or whomever. We demand the destruction of chaos and the re-establishment of order. But nobody is converted by power; rather, in the process individuals become expendable and are destroyed. Could we not see that within the chaos there is a divine word, the offer of something new if we are vulnerable enough to love? To incarnate this word, to make the new thing visible, is to cooperate with the realization of the word of God in this physical and conscious world. The Spirit of love brings life out of the waters of chaos. These are not the mere discoveries of physical science or psychology. They are available to everyone. It is a matter of the deep word of God which is present and must be found in all things and events. We find it in laughter and pain, in joys and sorrows, in life and in our death.

The Creator God has no cheap solutions for our problems and our chaos. Problems and chaos are the result of our being free. God does not prevent our hurt; hurt is the price of growth. Our tragedies do not prevent the beginning he made in us from reaching its end. We are called to bring our chaos to Christ and to realize that in our freedom and in creation's freedom to be and to grow, his covenant of love is being fulfilled. He promised to be with us always. He never promised to spare us the trials of freedom. He guides and sustains an emerging world; he does not drive it. There is little fixed order because we are a pilgrim people perpetually on the move. We never know what the next bend in the road will reveal—it is part of the chaos. Whatever it reveals, be it pleasant or painful, is a challenge to us to love and to choose. The Spirit empowers us to continue coming into being if we embrace the chaos.

MORAL CHAOS   I

I will begin with the story of a happening in a religious community of men in the midwest. It was early in the morning of December 8, the feast of the Immaculate Conception. The men were kneeling around in the dimly lit church doing the meditation prescribed by their rule. It was a sort of half-sleepy, half-spaced-out mental attitude of good will and warmth toward God and Mary. No particular reasoning was required.

Halfway through a young novice saw the light. He understood the Immaculate. He grasped, or was grasped by, the mystery of innocence. He got up quietly, went to the sacristy where he removed every stitch of his clothing and came out into the sanctuary before the altar. Stretching out his arms in full view of his startled brethren, he announced to all: "I am the immaculate conception." From their point of view it was accounted unto him as madness—our world not having a notion what to do with innocence. Should you doubt that, observe what we did to Jesus. That he removed his clothing, the facade, was insightful, as meaningful as his identifying completely with his understanding. He knew innocence because he was innocent. He was back to Adam. He was perhaps the first fully sane man in his community. He had an intuition of immaculate morality, and his mind and our culture could not cope with the insight. The chaos, which in his insight into original innocence he had for the moment transcended, broke like the ocean over his head and he was hustled off to a mental home. It is paradoxical but true of this world of ours that the innocent have to be crucified and the moral have to appear as being out of their minds.

For ourselves, the point is this: surrounded as we are by so many so-called sane people, people terribly well adjusted to this world's values, how are we going to remain faithful to our divine madness? If we stick with the old routines we will make no waves. There will not, indeed, be anything creative in our lives but people will praise us for being a value to society, productive, adding to the economy, law-abiding, trustworthy. But if we break out of the routine there will be chaos. Nothing creates so much chaos as suggesting that there might be a better way to do things, that any viewpoint is only one of several approaches, or that the old ways work no more. There is a proverb, a bit of folk-wisdom coming out of a naive approach to life which says: "In the country of the blind the one-eyed man is king." Presumably he can keep an eye on things. In a highly organized society, a world-enclosed-on-itself, this is totally false. In the kingdom of the blind the man who has even partial vision is seeing things, hallucinating. He is suggesting that there is something out there that the empirical evidence of all others proves to be non-existent. He is disrupting the whole order of things, troubling people, being untrustworthy, creating unrest and chaos, and must be hustled off. He is even suggesting that in the country of the blind moral-living people need not wear loincloths. Why cannot he leave us alone in the dark where we had a warm, if sleepy, relationship with God? Why stir things up now? The answer is that God's creative Spirit is restless within people, that he will never allow us to settle down in routine. The challenge of his presence within change and chaos will rouse us to get up and go. There will always be some chaotic person with one eye open.

Point No. 1: Moral chaos results from the universality of the presence of entropy in our world.

The energy of the universe is always changing its form. Entropy is a measure of the capacity of a system to undergo spontaneous change, a measure of the randomness, disorder and chaos in a system—any system—your furnace, your Church or your moral life. Law and order are not the condition of the world in which we live; chaos is, change is. From our logical, rational, orderly point of view a change in the routine order of things is chaos, especially when it happens spontaneously and against our will. Change is seen as disintegration. Yet the fundamental condition of our world, and therefore in the eyes of God the correct condition, is that things are falling apart. They are never falling together except in the long view of God. If there is order we must assume that it has been painfully built up, that somebody must have worked at establishing or imposing it. Let me give an example: If you had a truckload of bricks neatly stacked in a cube 6' × 6' × 6', how often would you have to dump the load out on the ground before it fell into another orderly cube? The answer is that it would never happen. Things fall apart. Put your brick building up and immediately change will begin to occur. In a matter of time utter chaos will take over. Change is our way of life. Energy must always be restored. Without change we have only death. This law of fragmentation is fundamental and universal. It is part of the chaos of the world. It is to be found in moral as well as in material matters. Our morality must constantly be built up, our moral energy restored. The fragmentation and falling apart of our moral life is a natural and fundamental condition of our humanness. Here we can say that entropy is the measure of the loss of our moral energy. A new order of behavior may be painfully built up out of the chaos, but from the moment it has been established the process of chaos begins all over again. Indeed, were there no chaos there would be no reason to make a moral choice or make a decision. There would be no progress either, no leap of faith, no risk of love— nothing but the dead-end of stoics or robots.

Within the chaos we have to be taught how to make a moral choice, we have to have informed consciences. But the idea that people as a whole will ever be fully taught or fully informed is a miracle of imagination thought up by a moral professor somewhere. We make the best decisions we can with whatever facts we have got. And most of our facts are not discovered in church or in books but from our peer group. We are moral or immoral because the people we admire are such, not because someone has got it down in a book. Unaware of your personal initiation into the moral life, and running the risk of boring you, I will now, to illustrate this point, set down in a few words, as my memory serves me, an accurate and faithful account of my own initiation into the realm of moral behavior. I was thirteen years of age when, with a group of other boys, I entered boarding school. We were all rather innocent. We had not as yet received any formal training in morality. What morality we had was gained from observing our parents, who were very upright people. The switch from a simple family life to life in a boarding school presented us with tensions and challenges not previously encountered. We reacted to the chaos with no great fraternal love. We became adept at inflicting mental pain on one another, taunting each other for physical and mental limitations, thoroughly disliking several of our priest-teachers. It was at this point that our formal initiation into Catholic morality took place. What we most needed at the time was to learn how to cope with the taunting and the mental pain, with physical abuse in the classroom, without losing our Christian love. That is not what we got.

What happened was this: within six months of our arrival a Holy Ghost Father came to conduct our retreat. He felt it his obligation to enlighten us all on the sinfulness of sexual behavior, it being the only immorality worth considering. It was an area in which we were all rather innocent. We had not heard the subject mentioned at home. We knew the basic facts of life, of course, embellished with some raunchy fantasies. But, curiously, we never connected it with sin. The Father, discreetly and in private, began the conversation with each of us by asking if we knew of a part of the body that got stiff. We nodded our heads solemnly and replied, "Yes, Father," while inwardly thinking, "For crying out loud, what the hell is he getting at?" He then went on to inform us that any playing around in that area was mortal sin for which we would be damned and go to hell. That was it. When we emerged one by one from the interview we compared conversations and swapped some cruder insights into the whole affair. But when little Joey, who was twelve, told us that he had replied by asking, "Do you mean a cramp, Father?" he was greeted with cheers of sheer delight. The trouble from there on out was that it would be possible to hate others without any consciousness of sin, for it was evidence of manliness. Serious sin was found only in the area of sexuality.

Be that as it may, the fact of our ignorance in this area in no way diminished the liveliness of our discussions. On the contrary it enabled the most heroic and grotesque suppositions to be presented for consideration. In Ireland, facts have never been allowed to debase the art of conversation anyway. But it was all talk. In five years of boarding school I never once witnessed any sexual impropriety.

Talk, however, was something else. It was a sort of responsibility. Tom declared that the innocence of one of the boys named Dennis was altogether unhealthy. Dennis had a round ruddy face, not unlike a harvest moon. He was serious and studious. He seldom smiled and never on any occasion uttered a four-letter word. Tom announced to the class that since Dennis' innocence was based on ignorance he felt that it was his obligation to instruct him. The class agreed that something had to be done to save him, but they knew that it would be a contest. During the break between classes Tom would pour a steady stream of sexual information into Dennis' ear. Some of it was crude, of course, but most of it was outrageously funny. Dennis never blinked an eye, never once smiled when everybody else was cracking up, never gave a sign that he even heard it. He would solemnly read his book or converse with The Miss who sat the other side of him. The Miss got his name from his delicate ways and unfailing good manners but was a very strong personality. This went on pretty regularly for five years. Then came the weeks of our Leaving Certificate examination.

On afternoons when there was no examination, we would go on group walks into the country, and on our return there would be cookies and cocoa in the refectory. There was no obligation to go on the walk. One could remain in the study hall on the fourth floor and "swat" the books. Dennis always remained there. The trouble was that when we got back from the walk we would devour the cookies and cocoa in a matter of minutes, before anyone in the study hall even knew we had returned. It was on one of those afternoons that some prankster entered the study hall and announced that we were in the refectory. Dennis immediately jumped up and rushed down the four flights of stairs to the refectory, only to find it locked and nobody there. His face flushed with anger and he came charging up the stairs two at a time. Halfway up he met the president of the school, a severe man with hunched shoulders, hooked nose and a face as sharp as a knife. He was known to the students as Crump. "Ah, my great God, Dennis, what is the hurry?" asked Crump with annoyance. Dennis, who had almost run into him, looked up with blazing eyes and said, "I thought they were in from the f------ walk." "Great God, Dennis, what is that I heard you say?" replied the president. He then went on to inform Dennis that the entire class was a group of moral degenerates, that there were only two in the class who had been found worthy of receiving the annual gift of hand missals given to the graduates, Dennis and The Miss, and that now Dennis himself was disqualified.

Tom had a point. A morality based on ignorance is of no value to anybody. At best it would leave a person infantile. We are not really born innocent. It has to be achieved—brick by brick, so to speak. Christian innocence is a strength that can withstand martyrdom, but it is gained at the price of a great deal of struggle within a great deal of chaos. Too often we have confused the inner and outer chaos with sin. We have looked at the moral entropy and said it was also sin and we have left people with an unnecessary sense of guilt. St. Paul mentions his own sense of chaos in Romans 7: "I fail to carry out the things I want to do, and I find myself doing the very things I hate. . . . Who will rescue me from this body doomed to death? The grace of God through Jesus Christ our Lord." When Dennis called the walk what he called it, everybody felt that he had arrived at a basic honesty in which he could express his feelings as they truly were. Nobody thought that he had been corrupted or that Tom ever intended to corrupt him. And everybody felt fine about being unworthy of the hand missals. Morality cannot be bought at the price of one's humanness.

Point No. 2: Moral chaos arises from the need we have to transcend ourselves coupled with our ignorance of how to go about it.

People have a hunger to transcend themselves. Ultimately, it is a hunger for God, Absolute Transcendence. This hunger is most noticeable in our high school years. In later years we settle down, become complacent and self-satisfied and wish to impose our self-security on the young in the guise of morality. All the hot-rodding around, the compulsions to take chances, the thrills and spills, the rebelliousness against restraint is an effort to taste transcendence. When young people tell us, "Man, it's out of this world," they are giving expression to a fundamental need for what is greater than this world. Their chaotic exploits are often more honestly moral than our sense of righteousness. The opposition of youth to institutions and to law and order is not so much disrepect for order as opposition to an attitude to life that eliminates the spontaneous, creative, mystical and transcendent elements in it that should be their heritage. One might question what the institution does to foster the mystical

24

element in life which people most deeply need to be fully human. Ninety percent that goes for sin among the youth is simply their mistakes in hassling with inner and outer chaos. That does not mean that sin does not exist. It does, wherever there is malicious intent to inflict injury, wherever others are treated as objects. But we should hardly be in too great a hurry to assume a malicious intention. Even then, it is a curious fact that a person who has enough determination to sin willfully has within that very determination the will power to change and become a saint. The lives of the saints are full of this sort of thing. Most of us who "are neither hot nor cold," with the determination to be neither outright sinners, nor great saints, are in greater danger from our very indifference.

Point No. 3: Moral chaos arises out of the fact that we who are called to live an "ideal" are ourselves less than ideal people.

When the Church preaches morality—as indeed it must, but not to the extent of forgetting the mystical life of Christ in us—it upholds an ideal. What else could we expect it to uphold? It cannot, after all, preach some sort of compromise. But the teaching Church knows even better than we do that people are not ideal. The Church has a long history and a long memory. We are broken, fragmented, weak, blinded by all kinds of psychological blocks and emotional compulsions. At times we are just plain lonely or fearful. It is perfectly fine to proclaim an ideal: people should live in peace and justice, marriage should not end in divorce, priests should be celibate, concubinage and polygamy should cease in Africa, there should be no abortions, no stealing, no war. It is an ideal from which a large section of humanity falls short, and that very frequently from no willful fault of their own. It is absolutely a waste of time saying that if they listened and shaped up they very well could live the moral law. They couldn't. Most people live in the midst of moral chaos. They know perfectly well that they err; they seldom need to be told. So, then, should we preach some sort of compromise, a lowest common denominator that everybody can observe? No. A world enclosed on itself will do that for us. The ideal from which we fall short is there to challenge and inspire us. But only the individual tries to live it—the "just man who falls seven times a day." Even good people are sinners. And they did not change their behavior and

25

become good people because somebody told them they were wrong. Somewhere somebody uncovered the good that was already within them. Somebody informed by word or example how utterly loved they were by God for their own sakes, not for their performance. Only when somebody convinces us that the beginnings and framework of the ideal are already within us will we begin to reach out for it. God alone is the Absolute Ideal.

Point No. 4: Moral chaos arises from confusing the concept of "right and wrong" with that of "loving and unloving."

What it boils down to is this: our religion is not a religion of "right and wrong" but a religion of "loving or unloving." The question facing us in any decision within chaos is not: "Is this the right thing to do or is it wrong?" That is a Greek, not a biblical approach. The question is: "Is this form of behavior loving or unloving?" Down through the centuries we have fought crusades, gone to court, excommunicated and hurt people because of our "rights." This was the so-called "right" thing to do. In point of fact most of it was very unloving. In the name of the "right" thing to do, and in forcibly imposing the right behavior, we have destroyed individuals who simply, and by virtue of the broken human condition, could not measure up. We have to allow the chaos to continue and love people in their brokenness. There is absolutely no possibility of ending the chaos. God loves people the way they are today— dammit, why can't somebody tell them? Tomorrow he will love them the way they shall be tomorrow. People respond to love; they have a secret resistance to what is imposed. The very intrinsic freedom of the individual resists the presumption of those who would organize their lives. But they are willing to do the utmost to respond to one they know genuinely loves them. They find it impossible to respond to one who knows what is "right" for them. It is important that people be taught how unselfishly they are loved by God. How else will they ever respond to him? Morality is only a by-product that flows out of loving and being loved. It is always secondary to the mystical life of grace. It cannot be imposed without that love except through fear. We are fearful of the great organizers in our lives. It is in no way proper that they should make us fearful of God.

In view of the struggles the little ones have to live the moral life,

I was saying to my friend, Father Bill, the other day that it would be a good thing if the higher clergy had to spend a year back in the logging towns of the Wilderness Area. It would give them an experience of loneliness, of cultural privation—a first-hand look at the struggles of people to survive. I suggested that a whole new compassionate approach to life might result from it since power, prestige and material security inevitably corrupt us. He replied by saying that there was a flaw in my reasoning. Those kind of people, he said, would never be stuck in the Wilderness Area. They would not be three months there before being brought into the city because they are the great organizers. Wherever there is a social system of any kind there have to be organizers and administrators. Somebody has got to run it and be responsible for it. It, it, it. Organization means power and power has to be exercised. I suggested that the only power Christ ever had was to lay down his life for others, that ministry is service. The decision-making of those in power is also a service, he replied, but it has to be done with love. The chaos remains. All people are called to right behavior, but not all right behavior is loving; therefore all should be comfortable with the chaos. It is a perfectly chaotic syllogism.

This is a sufficiently long section and I notice a note of crankiness creeping in. Within the freedom granted in chaos I will continue the matter in the following chapter. Moreover, it is four o'clock in the afternoon, the sky has clouded up, I have a pimple on the left side of my nose, and I am tired of it all.

MORAL CHAOS   II

Point No. 5: Moral chaos arises out of the mistaken notion that ideal behavior can be successfully enforced.

Trying to enforce moral behavior only adds to the chaos. Many good people I know are spiritual schizophrenics as a result of this enforcement. They are unable to acknowledge that they are ever in the wrong lest in acknowledging it they might be punished by God. They also hate their guilt which makes them punish themselves. The situation now becomes a matter of taking a risk. They must take the risk of believing that God would continue to love them even though they are terribly in the wrong. But they continue to protect themselves against God and self-loathing because all they were ever taught was that God is the stern upholder of the moral law, the One who punishes. This leaves them in a hopeless bind. To win God's approval (which does not have to be won) they feel that their conduct must be perfect, but on the other hand they find themselves incapable of perfection. Someday they are going to have to surrender and allow their sinful imperfect selves to be loved just as they are. They are going to have to be at peace with the chaos. They are going to have to find out that God's love for them is not measured by their conduct. The imposition of moral imperatives upon them under the threat of punishment has put them on a huge guilt trip. Many do not risk the surrender of their lives to God until they are on their deathbed. When people in high office demand so much of weak broken people they should be aware that they might possibly have a blind spot themselves. It results from an abstract approach to morality and partially from their own success in life. Perhaps, not having tasted the shame of recognized moral failure, they themselves have never had to make any notable surrender in love to God. People are not asking for fine distinctions in moralizing but for compassion, understanding and encouragement. Let us humbly admit that moral behavior has been demanded with some heavy insistence. And the higher the office of the upholder of morality, the more ready he should be to apologize and admit mistakes. It is not too much to expect the risk of humility in religious leaders.

Point No. 6: Moral chaos arises from the fact that the power to do good brings with it a corresponding power to do evil.

Every gift has its shadow—it is part of the chaos. Power has oppression, love has possessiveness, virtue has pharisaism, ministry has recompense, success has vanity. We do not simply have power, love, virtue or service to others. Each one is had within the attraction of its opposite. And unless we have the heroic virtue of the saints we can accept the fact that the exercise of our gift is slightly tainted, to say the least. This should not at all prevent us from using that gift. It is part of the chaos that the greater the opportunity we have to do good, the greater is the danger of misusing that opportunity. Each advancement in knowledge and technology brings with it a corresponding power to misuse the knowledge. Nothing is static in this world of ours. Everything has within it the power to attract or to repel, to establish some attitude, presence or relationship or to self-destruct.

This does not mean that the world is a trap set by God to trip us up. It simply means that nothing can come to full rest without resting in its opposite. Everything is called continuously beyond itself. If you have a power to do good you also have a temptation: to fail to do it. But the temptation is only a time of crisis in which you are called to go beyond present limitations to a higher level of humanness. It is not something destructive but a dilemma. The purpose of the chaos is that we make a choice to move upward. The chaos fosters the essential humility we need to die to where we are at and surpass ourselves. Chaos is not moral corruption. It simply tells us that morality cannot be imposed and that others cannot make our decisions for us irrespective of how very much we need them to enlighten us.

If you will permit me I shall take up again my further initiation into becoming a moral person, a conscientious objector to violence and a decision-maker. During our high school years Flam taught us Latin, Johnny Pope—so-called from his bombastic manner—taught us Greek, and Wonky was our dean of discipline. Flam used a four-ply leather strap as an enabler to teach us Latin. He would remind us occasionally that the strap was part of the harness of a jackass. There was always silence before his classes, the silence of very real fear. Our knees and legs used to be trembling as we tried to memorize our Latin grammar before his class. We all had the same anxiety. Were you called to recite and made a mistake, he would grip you by the wrist with the palm of your hand upturned. You could not pull away. Then, holding the strap behind his shoulder with his other hand he would swing it forward and down on your palm twice. He would do the same with your other hand. Both hands would blow up like balloons. It was much worse if your were caught out at the blackboard. He would swing the strap full circle connecting it with your bottom at the end of the circle. Nobody dared protest. Protests would get you nowhere. And Latin was obligatory. Several years later this man's car broke down in the middle of an Irish bog. It seems that he got out of the car and tried to cross the bog toward a light in the distance. He never made it, and died of exposure. He was a pale asthmatic man, never in very good health, which excused everything. When they found him he was wearing his coat inside out. There is a centuries-old idea in Ireland that you are liable to be led astray by the fairy folk and get lost in the bog at night. To deceive the Little People and turn away their powers you are supposed to remove your coat, turn it inside out and put it back on. It was a grim death for a strange man.

Johnny Pope had huge hands. He did not need a strap. He would wing you one across the side of the head and you would see stars. But one could decide not to take Greek. In view of an inevitable five years of being beaten across the head I decided, after three months of it, to drop out of the Greek class. The risk was calculated. I knew that he would beat me unmercifully if I did so but that it would be over in a few days. Then there would be five years during which I could sit at the back of the room and watch him beat the living daylights out of the rest of them who had the same option as I but did not use it. One morning I sat back there. When he entered he saw me immediately and said: "Boy, why are you sitting at the back of the class?" I replied that I was not taking Greek anymore. It was, in a way, a sort of personal affront to him. It also meant one fewer from whom he could draw his per capita bonus income. He called me up front and said that I should get in my desk so that class could continue. It was a tense moment. I refused. He then stood me before the class and facing himself. He placed one of his large feet on my insteps so that I could not pull away from him. He slammed me one across the right side of the head. "Now, boy, will you take Greek?" "No, Father." Then one across the left side. "Now, will you take Greek, boy?" "No, Father." It continued on like that. At one point he asked, "Boy, do you think I am an angel?" "No, Father." Even then I thought it was a bit funny. The beating continued for three-quarters of an hour. The next day he called me up again and the procedure continued in the same manner except that at one point he ordered me outdoors where I had to walk around a water pump forty times while the class counted. They were at the windows laughing at his very unfunny jokes. That hurt, but I realized that they had to play along with him or be beaten themselves. He threatened dire consequences if I circled the pump thirty-nine or forty-one times. At the end of the third day he was defeated. To save face he said, "Now, boy, ask permission not to take Greek." It had never been a question of asking permission. It would never have been granted and would have made one's resistance disobedience. "Father, may I cease taking Greek?" "You may," he replied. The victory was very sweet. And I had learned a great deal about decisions and morality, about right and wrong, loving and unloving.

Wonky did not teach any class. He was responsible for our observance of the rules of the establishment. We attributed his meanness to the fact that he had suffered from malaria during his years as a missioner in Africa. I had the naive notion that spending some years in Nigeria was a fairly heroic thing to do. I was actually puzzled: How could a man who had spent several years on the mission be cruel? For the slightest infraction of the rule, for example talking after bedtime, he would cane us or kick our behind. He would walk up and down during recreation period reading his prayers from his thick breviary. Then suddenly he would call you over, and keeping his finger in the place where he was reading he would slam you across the head with the book. It was a novel use of the book of the official prayers of the Church—a way, I presume, of using the breviary to improve our moral behavior. But there were other really great priests in that high school, men I deeply respected. From them I learned that the power to do good was real, and that the power to do evil, the shadow, could be controlled.

Point No. 7: Moral chaos arises from the fact that the range of possible choices is now so great that no moralist can list them all. We must decide and choose what will make us holy people.

Our technological society has vastly expanded the range of possibilities, and consequently the range of choices—good ones and bad ones. The possibilities for good and evil are now so expanded that all the facts can no longer be known. This is a good thing since it clearly demonstrates that a religion reduced to morality, or concerned in its witness for the most part with morality, just will not work. The moralist can no longer be there with all the answers to what people should or should not be doing. The formulation of norms of behavior cannot keep up with the rapid expansion of our range of choices. We are challenged within the chaos of choices to a deeper understanding of religion as a response to the living Christ.

The objective value on which we base our life is no longer the "do" and "don't" of moralists but the indwelling Spirit of Christ alive in the individual and in the community. We come to know what to do by observing Christ as head and purpose of creation. We are social. We live and grow in interaction and interdependence. This has to be moral living. Put biblically, it reads: "He is the vine and we are the branches," he "is the cornerstone and we are the living stones which form the temple of God," he is "the head and we are the members" of his body. From this body of Christ there comes a guiding voice for conscience. This guiding voice is seen clearly in those people who have "put on Christ." It is something that is lived by good and holy people, genuine Christians. It can never be more than merely referred to in the statements, norms, abstract decrees of moralists and Church leaders. The norm of behavior is not something written in a document or relayed through the press; it is the example that is given to us by the actions of saintly people. The wealthy admonishing the poor, the powerful admonishing the little ones, the celibates admonishing the married, the priests admonishing the sisters are all ludicrous. People do not respond to admonitions but to holiness, the holiness of their peers. In the many possible choices before us we must choose because a power rises up within us telling us what the loving thing is that we must do. Very often we do not have clear choices nor anybody to tell us the "rights" and "wrongs" of the matter. The crisis has to be resolved in our death to selfishness. It is not done with clenched teeth—stoics are less than human. Nor is it routine, as if to be good meant that we were all little angels. At best, we walk a stumbling path. We are asked by Christ, not to be "right" all the time but to be converted and to be holy, that is, to live by the indwelling Spirit he has given us.

Point No. 8: Moral chaos arises out of the clash that exists between the rights of the individual and the rights of society.

The individual is also social. But there is a tension between the individual and society. Does the individual exist for society, or society for the individual? The problem has not been settled.

As individual persons we experience within ourselves an inalienable freedom and privacy. We cannot forfeit that inner uniqueness without ceasing to be human. We have a dignity that is personal in contrast to all existing being. Society must support and further its personhood and freedom. We are not robots or machines. This personhood cannot be forcibly denied. It has to be respected as something that is not given by society but is the sacredness of the individual before there is ever the thought of society existing. In this respect the person is more than society and must, at times, when the dignity of human personhood is in question, say "no" to society.

On the other hand the individual is social and can never be a complete person apart from social interaction. The individual must support society, must give and take so that others may be complete. In this respect society is more than the individual. The individual is called upon to give of his time and person, of his work and possessions, of his freedom and future for the well-being of society. It should be clear that in any moral decision-making in these areas the opportunities for chaos are innumerable. Here are questions of taxes, housing permits, draft registration, warfare, business practices, religious obligations and other matters too many to mention. Society, especially when considered as sufficient to itself, is not the whole of reality. The free, private, and sacred individual is not the whole of reality. There is a tension situation out of which might come, not a solution, but insights as to how to live and grow.

Even with the best of all possible societies the individual may opt out into forms of alienation and refuse to grow in freedom. And even with the best of individuals, society may never be formed. Well-being cannot be imposed on individuals even by a benevolent form of civil or ecclesiastical government. Trying to do so is a form of tyranny. Society cannot solve the problem of personal growth. The Church as society can try to demand celibacy, monogamy, fidelity to religious commitment; it can rant about birth control, women in priesthood and out of religious garb, priests in politics and a hundred thousand other things of law and order, but it does so at the risk of stunting the Christian growth of individuals. I am not saying that it should not so speak to us. It should, while being mindful of its limits. And the individual must be responsible and aware of others and the goals and purpose of the Church or state. There is a situation of creative chaos. Something greater than both must set them free. It would have to be a creative force absolutely oriented in love for all. This can only be God's gift of himself which is made, not to the Church alone but to all people of good will. It enables us to walk in the way of Jesus, to be free to exist and be hurt, to recognize the benevolence of all reality and the foundation and purpose of reality, God.

Our opening on God does not always, or immediately, heal us of moral weakness, psychological blocks, cultural conditioning or misinformation. Even the saints had very real blind spots at times. The whole chaotic situation of moral confusion is here to stay. Confusion, struggle, failure, picking oneself up again, trusting the Father's love, caring about little ones, succeeding for a time, listening humbly to the crap about shaping up, loving, in tears at times, laughing, being ironic about the human mess, knowing there is mercy, accepting providence, gentling one's heart and bringing small beautiful moments into the world are all elements of our chaotic moral situation. "Who, then, can be saved?" It was an apostle who put the question. Christ has already reconciled the world to himself and sent the Holy

Spirit among us for the forgiveness of sins. Through the ministry of the Church there is pardon and peace. Accept it and let the moral chaos be. It is not the fundamental problem. The fundamental problem will always remain a world that is so self-absorbed it does not know how desperately it needs Christ.

PERSONAL CHAOS

Our purpose in life is not to become angelic, but fully human. The incarnation of the Son of God establishes, once and for all, that the fully human is the measure of holiness. It is the fully human that is in the image and likeness of God. The entire body-spirit person must be developed. It is not simply a matter of the spirit. Flesh and blood have gone into God in Christ and are holy. The overdevelopment of one aspect of our humanness to the neglect of the other is a distortion of reality. The humanness of God is a very real reality. But it is not easy to be fully human. We resist wholeness.

The chaos arises from the fact that there is both a unity and a distinction in the one person. We are paradoxical even to ourselves. We are masters in the art of creating our own chaos and it is perfectly all right. It is the way we are supposed to be. We also grow from the tensions we discover within ourselves if we dialogue with them. There is a unity: we are one person, spirit actualized and expressed through a physical body. And there is a distinction: the body places a limitation on the expression of our spirit both inwardly and outwardly. Inwardly we are limited in the free expression of thought, memory, love and creativity by the physical condition of our brain, chemical makeup and physical health. Because of the body we can only do a fraction of what is within the realm of possibility for the spirit. Outwardly the body limits us to this time and this space. What we have then is an integrated body-spirit person who is also a body versus spirit person. With our whole being we wish and decide to do something good, only to find that when we try to do so a conflict arises from some level of our makeup. As a unity a man may wish to express love, yet in doing so the spirit may wish to express it on one level, the body on another.

One attempted resolution to the problem is to restrict oneself to the one or to the other, to spirit to the rejection of the body, or to the body to the rejection of the spirit. There are fanatical ascetics, Christians, Moslem and Oriental, who starve themselves to death in the name of spirit, as well as those who neglect the body in the notion that only spirit matters. Then there are hedonists who indulge every aspect of the sensual and reject any claim of spiritual development.

Another attempted solution to the body-spirit chaos is to try to live on two separated levels, having the best of both worlds. There are religious people who act very devoutly but on the other hand love power or possessions. Bible-thumping millionaires and power-pressuring religious leaders are to be found everywhere.

A third attempted solution is a false undialectical unity. Here there is no thought of rejecting the one in favor of the other. It is merely assumed without questioning it. Some body-building types or beach beauties would find little reason for time in church or in an art gallery. Such a stroll would add little to the muscles or the tan. But there is no thought of rejecting the spirit. The same is true in reverse of certain prayerful types who assume the body without questioning its needs. There is none of the healthy dialectical tension which we find in St. Paul's struggles.

There is actually no satisfactory solution, unless you consider the development and the discipline of both to be a solution. The resolution is in what comes out of the struggle with the chaos. Without the struggle we are either fanatics or sheep. Yet it is not the extreme but the fully human that is the measure of holiness. Human life is a gift to be celebrated as the revelation, in image and likeness, of the living God. It is not a task that should drive people to extremes. But the personal chaos continues and the search for what is fully human also continues.

During my third year of high school I decided that I wanted to become a priest. Part of the decision arose from the chaos in the body-spirit situation. I thought that "saving my soul" would be facilitated by going all out for religion. It was not the only factor in my decision. There were other, more redeeming ones. I was unaware at the time that people make the correct decision for the wrong reasons and live long enough to purify those reasons. I also did not know that those who wait until everything is correct and crystal-clear often wind up making no decision at all. I felt that if I joined a religious community which had lots of time for prayer I just might make it in the next world. I even had a sort of attraction for the prayer thing anyway. Now I know that it is not the soul that needs saving but the person, the greedy stinking old body-person or the beautiful seductive body-person as the case might be.

I went up to see Crump. He did not invite me into his room. I was in need of some really solid advice, or spiritual direction, or discernment of spirits since my groping for a vocation would determine the whole of my future. We settled the entire matter in two minutes, standing at the door of his room. "Father, I would like to be a priest ... ah ... maybe in some order that, ah, does some praying ... maybe like the Dominicans or Franciscans or something." Nobody had ever joined the Dominicans or Franciscans from our high school. It was a sort of exotic suggestion. "I don't know anything about the Dominicans or Franciscans," he replied. "Why don't you join the Vincentians? Some of our students have gone there." I replied that I did not want to join the Vincentians because they were too like diocesan priests and I did not want to be a diocesan priest. "Oh, go on up to All Hallows," he said. "It's a good seminary." It was very clear from his body-language that the conversation was closed. All Hallows was for the diocesan clergy who would leave the country to serve in the English-speaking world. "All right, Father. Thank you." So it was settled. I felt I had done all that could be done. I did not want to be too picky about it. I went to All Hallows and got myself ordained as a diocesan priest.

This is what I mean by personal chaos. You have an inner crisis. You go with it to somebody for advice, and that person has neither the wisdom nor the interest to be of help. So you wind up not simply with a dumb opinion when opinions were not being sought, but with accepting the opinion—there being no other direction available. Direction is not a matter of getting another's opinion. It uncovers the validity or invalidity of your own opinion. And if you are sixteen, how are you to distinguish your head from the hole in it anyway? Nobody argued with Crump. It just was not done. However, this is God's world and there is a divine providence underlying all our decisions which will draw us toward salvation, with the result that with some measure of honesty things work out in the end. This is a far cry from saying something daft such as this being the will of God and that he had planned it like that all along. God does not have plans up his sleeve that we are unable to discover. We are free to be our own persons. We are floundering around in blissful chaos, the chaos that makes freedom possible, and we make the best, the second-best or a rotten choice, not knowing half the time which is which. It is then that a loving God adjusts his grace and protection to us wherever we have gotten ourselves. There is no fixed, predetermined plan of God for our lives. He respects our chaos as we grow toward a mature personal freedom. He is with us, just that. And his being with us is at least the beginnings of our salvation here and now.

In All Hallows the first serious question asked of me within the first month was where I wished to go after ordination. I told the rector that I wished to go to England. I felt that since the choice was offered to me it was all right to wish to be close to home. He wrote my intention down in a ledger of sorts. Two months later I was called into his office. He told me that the bishop of Fresno, California wanted some priests and asked if I would go. There was very little choice in the matter. I hesitated, assessing the situation, reckoning the consequences of turning it down and wanting to do what I thought God was asking of me. But there were no heroics in my intentions. "Well," I replied hesitantly, "I don't mind." He wagged his finger back and forth rapidly and said, "Yes or no, yes or no, yes or no." "Yes," I said. "Good man, good man, good man," he replied. "Send in Mr. . ." naming another student. Well, here I was, the one who wanted to be a friar or a monk, launched on my way to saving my soul and signed up for the diocese of Fresno, California. Other than having some sort of notion where California was, we had no notion where Fresno was located. Nobody would say that the decision to go there was not my own choice, nor would I say it myself. I would go no further than saying that it would take God to unravel the reasons for our decisions and the influences brought to bear on them. I would say further that the Holy Spirit is the Alka-Seltzer of the body of Christ. That he succeeds is clearly obvious from the fact that so many of us love this body in spite of the corruptible elements in its institutional makeup.

There is a point I am making here about personal chaos. It is this: that advice and discernment are hard to come by; that the decisions we make can, with the guaranteed grace of God, work to our advantage in ways we had not anticipated; that we really have less reason than we think for complaining about the decisions we made in the past, or about the influences that were brought to bear on them; that our thrust must be to look constantly to the future and find out what new and creative thing we might bring out of our personal chaos. Four years after I got to Fresno I did what I always wanted to do and joined the monks, but the struggle to be fully human continues. It gets more subtle, not more manageable.

The ingredients that form our personal chaos are more or less common to all: inner struggle, survival, messing up our successes, triumphing even in our defeats, revulsions, surprises, love and hate, death of loved ones, the logical and the incongruous. There are other more serious matters that weigh on our minds: wars, famines, atrocities, fears, nuclear weapons, the exploitation of the weak and powerless. They cause anguish in our hearts. In all of these we are confronted with evil, the evil inseparable from a world closed on itself. There is nothing petty about our personal chaos if we realize our place in the world and the challenge to be fully human. Evil is a reality. It has to be contained. We have no right to be totally passive about it. Evil reveals itself in violence. To contain it grace has to be equally violent even if in a reverse form. The good and unselfish decisions we make about life do violence to us. There is no other way. Christ told us he did not bring peace but the sword, a sword that separates us from many things we hold dear. He told us to carry his cross and our own. That too is violence to our natures. He said that "the kingdom of heaven suffers violence and the violent take it by storm" (Mt. 11:12).

So the response we make to God within our personal chaos is not a pious, cultural, Sunday-morning feeling—which is not to say that such comfort should be disdained. It is to say that religion is not some wishy-washy moralizing comfort for our psychological problems. It is the violence of grace that we see in the prophets, the sweat of terror on Christ in Gethsemani, the cries and tortures of the martyrs, the anguish of people who have given all for Christ. The offer of grace and favor is often made within repugnance, humiliation and personal weakness. The power that others exercise on us and our own powers are, in the end, only a charade. It is the power of God that counteracts evil in our world, for all that he works through people. Only God can save the world. And even if in our stupidity we bomb the enemy flat we still cannot bomb what he is thinking. The chaos remains.

On the one hand, the world is a "new creation," beautiful, honestly desirable and necessary. On the other hand, it is an illusion to think that in grasping for all that we can control of it we shall be happy. It is the genius of the Church that it tempers this grasping. It is also its genuis that it tempers the violence of grace. One need know very little of the spiritual movements in the history of the Church to appreciate the need for discipline in grace-filled situations. The lives of the saints, to say nothing of lesser enlightened people, are filled with examples of grace-filled extravagances and grace-initiated compulsions. The very grace of God itself churned up their personal chaos. But it is the weakness of the Church to be overcautious. Overcontrol, in the name of prudence, can emasculate the gift and kill the spirit. The violence of the Spirit, the taking of the kingdom by storm, cannot be reduced to prudence and to taking no risks. Our personal chaos, which has no absolute solution, tells us to take risks. Christ took risks and the blood of Christ was no imprudence. The martyrs also took risks and their blood was no imprudence.

Another aspect of our personal chaos is this: the evil is within us. It is not within us objectified like a tumor. It is found within us where the good is found, in our will, in our spirit. It is a sort of twist in our will, a wrinkle. The very will which chooses good also finds itself resisting and rejecting it. It would be all very well if we could say that the evil was an objectified thing out there somewhere, an evil-in-general, that it was possible to blame it on others or on circumstances. But the evil leaves us all flawed personalities even if we never did what is wrong. It is a twist in the will of a saint as it is in a sinner. Evil activity is the activity of individuals. It may seem a force out there because people conspire together to do what is wrong. That is why the Church is not fighting evil-as-such. Evil-as-such is an abstraction. Christ has settled the problem of evil-as-such. The Church proclaims to this aspect of our personal chaos the word and work of Christ as the way out of our personal impasse. Living the mystery of Christ is personal; the life that happens to us is personal;

the special grace that each one of us receives is personal; our struggle with evil is personal. The chaos within which we live, struggle and become holy is the element of God's freedom within which we choose to be who we want to be. This says that the body-spirit person who is good and has a secret longing for what is bad, who is holy and is allured by what is evil, lives out his or her life always surprised, even in the act of sin, by the grace of Christ which eventually makes us whole.

If you have been touched by the grace of God, if you have not played religion as a cultural comforting thing but have fought the good fight, then you have experienced chaos in your personal life. It has been the struggle of knowledge with ignorance, of strength with weakness, of evil with holiness—your evil with your holiness. You have also experienced the evil and holiness in others—in your family, community, Church and state. In your personal chaos you have been at war. It is a deadly war fought for your humanness, for your salvation. You probably have scars, and by now you have either survived—not succeeded—or you have allowed yourself to be defeated. If you have survived you still have faith, and a compassion for those who hurt you. But bitterness does not become you—not bitterness at others, not at yourself. You were born with your flaws; you did not choose them. You must accept your scars with humble dignity. You do not have to deny that they exist. Christ's scars were there after resurrection. The outcome of your chaos has already been decided in Christ. No one defeats you unless you defeat yourself, and bitterness is the pettiest defeat of all. Your chaos was personal. So will be your vindication.

ART AND CHAOS

We are all artists to some degree. We have a skill no matter how prosaic it may be. We project images in words and deeds that reveal our concept of reality. We are each within our own person a special kind of artist. It is an area that bears examination.

Somebody once quoted Pythagoras to the effect that "the function of art is to impose order on chaos." The reference was not supplied. Even if he did so write, we must remember that Pythagoras was a mathematician and must be allowed his little prejudice. It is a sort of half-truth. A work of art must have symmetry, balance, harmony, a "unity in multiplicity." It would seem, indeed, to take disparate elements and set them in order in a work "which on being seen pleases." But many people are not pleased at all by modern art and feel that it is sheer chaos. A few would say that the function of art is to interpret the prevailing chaos. Most artists would agree with Nabokov that art merely portrays truthfully what it sees. It "holds the mirror up to nature." It reflects truthfully our modern chaos. Most artists would proclaim loudly that art has no function at all, that function is a tin can you tie to a donkey's tail. Art needs no justification. Its purpose is fulfilled in being well crafted. Truth does not need a function to justify it. In much the same way, the mystic, brother of the artist, prays for the sake of praying, not for purposes. Commercialism belongs neither in the work of the artist nor in that of the mystic. They have bypassed the world of functionaries.

Art cannot abolish chaos. It abolishes nothing. Perhaps as a symbol it brings things together, the observer and his world, and without abolishing the chaos enables the observer to live more fully despite its presence. It is a catalyst that provokes a catharsis in that it relieves tension and anxiety by bringing repressed material to consciousness. Mystical prayer has much the same effect. Both artist and mystic proclaim that it is possible to live in the midst of chaos and not be overcome by it. In the midst of chaos both artist and mystic have the inspiration of truth and "the ability to make something according to the right course of reason." Both follow through on an intuition that basically comes from love, that is, from the surrender each makes of himself to the object of his contemplation.

One might say, with some irony, that it takes great artistry to create a magnificent chaos. Great reformers and revolutionaries might be cited. Most of us do not have it in us. But the artist who has genius as well as talent produces a new thing. Art fosters creativity. Precisely because it is new there are no rules by which to assess it. It is a break with the past, a leap of intuition. Nobody other than the artist can judge it as being true or false to his insight. Because it is new it demolishes the old laws and principles. Since it breaks with convention it must, of necessity, have the appearance of chaos. This explains why some of the world's finest music, painting, architecture and other art forms took years before they were appreciated. When Mahler's First Symphony was performed for the first time in June 1894, the German press denounced it as a crime against law and order in symphonic music. Handel's Messiah could not find a stage until it came to Dublin. Synge's *Playboy of the Western World* caused a riot in the streets of Dublin on the first night of its production. People snickered at Picasso, and clerics have had hacks paint over the nude masterpieces of Michelangelo. There are no rules of good order to govern the new creation until others begin to imitate it. Then it becomes itself the norm. Imitators, or those inspired by the new form, will surpass or fall short of it. The new movement will be assimilated into the accepted and convential, and order will flourish again for a time. But art is restless, refusing to be confined. A new form and a new chaos will emerge again and the process will continue.

The chaos is not only created by the new art forms; it is also the fertile soil out of which the art emerges. We are dealing with the presence of mystery in things which can never be measured by norms or order. Basically, we are dealing with the deepest levels of our being. They defy neat explanations. Art emerges from this mystery and in turn moves those deepest levels. It enables us to know ourselves and urges us toward healing and transcendence. In that sense all art can be said to be religious. The artist, like the mystic, is moved by the Spirit. He or she makes the invisible world of mystery visible. This world of mystery, with its welter of possibilities, is the ground out of which the artist mines new forms. This invisible, scarcely felt or understood world of ours hungers for the true, the good and the beautiful. It hungers also for the sacred. The artist uncovers this hunger, whets the appetite and for a time satisfies it. For that reason art is an explosive medium. It sits in judgment on all that is untrue, unjust and ugly in life. It is courted and feared by both Church and state. They are aware that, more than any other medium, it can move people to action. It can be used against them. So they want to censor and control it. They do not wish the judgment of art upon themselves, the power it has to expose the spirit, to reveal the superficial and cruel in what is corrupt in their institutions. They would rather use it as a weapon of propaganda for their own purposes, to control the thinking of their members. Art emerges from this chaos, and causes chaos.

It is not the laws that control people's thinking. Laws only control our behavior. Our thinking is controlled more by the haphazard chaos in our lives and the pleasures and pains resulting from it. The human spirit resists control for the simple reason that we instinctively know that we are made for absolutes, freedom and transcendence. We are moved into action far more by the pleasures and pains than by any control exercised by law. Should a friend die by violence we do not think of the excellent legal system we have; we cry out at life, and no law can comfort us. Now it is pleasure and pain which are the grist for the mill of art. Without them art would never survive. The pain and outrage expressed in art have brought down governments. There is a power in literature and song to form the thinking of a nation. The fight for freedom has always gone back to the culture of the people to find its inspiration and justification. Art, and not law, expresses in a moment, in a glance, the pain and hunger that people feel. It moves them to demand fulfillment. The unverbalized ideas born of pleasure and pain and presented in art control how people think at their deepest level. True art brings those depths to the surface demanding that we be honest and religious people. It challenges us to discover and act upon the real meaning of our existence. The reverse is also true: when we are denied what is of artistic merit we are forced to live on a superficial self-obsessed level.

The work of art must be moral, even if the artist himself suffer from moral chaos. It must be true, competent, inspiring and appealing to our intellect as well as to our senses. If it portrays an untruth it must do so truly as untruth. It may never portray the untrue as true. What is immoral or untrue, what exploits people or circumstances, can never move the deepest levels of our being into transcendent greatness. Bad art, or great technique put to bad uses, gives no glory to God and no help to humanity. It is the revelation of spirit that makes for great art, and spirit is absent from what is immoral or untrue.

Today, art is associated in the minds of most people with beauty, with aesthetics. Formerly, it was primarily associated with utility and knowledge, the free skills and products of industry and the mind—the so-called industrial and liberal arts. In an earlier age the person who could "make a good thing well" was an artist, and the work accomplished was a work of art. What was perfectly true to its purpose, honest and sincere in its craftmanship, was artistic. It might have been a good piece of pottery, or a chair, or a barn, or a folk melody. A barn could be a work of art because it was well crafted, honest and sincere in expression and true to its purpose. On the other hand a great mansion might fail the test because it manifested the vanity and vulgarity of its builder. The work of art was the apt outward expression of what was in the mind and understanding of all the people. It was a concrete expression of a form meaningful to them or an apt symbol of a value around which they centered their lives. And it had to work. If it was a sword it had to cut; if it was a piece of pottery it had to be able to hold things for storage or for cooking. If the value, for example, was fertility the symbol had to look fertile and be able to draw people to cult. Sweet sentimentality had no place in their art objects.

Most of these art objects emerged from need, from some form of stress or from chaos in the life of the artist. They rarely emerged from pure leisure. It was the need that produced the pottery, the chair or the barn. The folk melodies were often composed to please a patron. The life of Michelangelo was one of intolerable chaos, his work pressured by the need to fulfill the demands of Julius II and other patrons. Patrons of the arts are a necessary motivating force. They wreak havoc on the sensitive and emotional lives of their proteges, but without their demands much of the world's greatest art would never have been created. The artistic temperament is notably volatile since the artist is terribly aware and sensitive to the world about him. The chaos of impressions which he receives may bring him to the brink of mental disorder. Yet out of this, as for example in the writings of Dostoevesky or the paintings of Van Gogh, comes a worldview portrayed in a way that otherwise would never have existed. Beethoven struggled with his deafness. It is painful to think that he never heard the Ninth Symphony. Mozart and Rembrandt experienced the chaos caused by poverty and unpaid bills. Others struggled with tragedy in their personal lives. Out of all this chaos came an expression of life and of the human spirit from which we have all benefited.

About the time of the Renaissance, the "fine arts"—those intended primarily for beauty alone—were cut off from the more humble crafts. They were accorded a certain prestige. They became a status symbol of wealth and the privilege of the so-called upper classes. They were seen as belonging to cultured people. The masses of people lost touch with art, but because they had an innate hunger for it they devoured, and continue to devour, bad productions. Church and state have not hesitated to supply them with oceans of hideous material, and the people themselves have defended the junk with all the passion and self-consciousness of those who have been led to believe that they have no culture. The piously sentimental and the grossly materialistic became the norms of people's tastes. Mass production in plastic and plaster of paris removed every last vestige of spirit. The State, as in Russia, commissioned horrendous works of sculpture to commemorate the working man and to celebrate achieved quotas. The armies came up with martial music with which to drum the military into war. And here at home, on the Feast of the Holy Cross in 1980, someone baked a cake in the form of a cross, covered it with icing and curlicue decorations with pink flowers in the center, and gave it to our community. Someone pointed to it and said: "The triumph of the Holy Cross." Another said: "How sweet it is, how sweet it is." And a third said: "It just goes to prove that the cross is a piece of cake."

Meanwhile, the elite feel they know what the rules and norms of beauty are, even if for the person who knows beauty there are no rules. The elite concentrate on the abstract, on the "canons of beauty" which must be imposed. Art dies for lack of spirit, but a few artists continue on. In a pragmatic society art is gently mocked in deference to those who think it is useless. Wealthy men buy it as an investment and hide it behind guard dogs and electric fences. Artists are not supported by patrons in the Church or in the state. They wander off into dead ends—dead because whatever the merit of their work it has virtually no impact on society at large.

Having an impact on society and being functional are two different things. Chaos arises when people insist that the art work be functional. "What good is it?" they ask. "What use can you put it to?" An art object can be useful without being used. It is to be celebrated, enjoyed, contemplated. The millionaire collector sees its function in appreciating in value in a time of inflation. But the artist "makes a good thing well" and puts on it the impress of his spirit. The knowledge of things is not sufficient without the knowledge of how to make the thing. He is an accomplished craftsman. He leaves the discussion of aesthetics to the elite. He himself is humble. He is nobody's functionary. A hydrogen bomb is functionary. It also inspires awe, raises questions about the meaning of life, is well crafted. We should have one erected in every city square so that it might have the right impact on society. How frustrating it must be that the artist of the bomb cannot display his work and the functionary cannot drop it. The artist cannot be responsible for what others do with his work. Is a Ming vase less an art work because you never place flowers in it? What about an electric chair? Designing electric chairs could be a powerful medium, while their use would reveal the insanity that still lingers with us. I am getting cynical. Can the chaos ever be avoided? Is it not the place of freedom, the place where we make choices to better the world in which we live?

Our imagination which presents us with so much chaos is also the seat of all creativity. From the imagination the artist projects images. The painter does not paint what he sees with his eyes, a photographic-style reproduction, but what he sees with his spirit. Art is a language in images and symbols by which the artist communicates with us in perceptual terms, not in concepts. He clarifies, dramatizes and intensifies the world about him as he reveals it to us. The imagination of the artist will reveal not only the harmony but also the very real chaos in the world. He will remind us of how responsible we are for this world of ours, how well or maliciously we use it. Since the artist, more than others, experiences the paradoxes in the world he has to discipline his imagination so that his image will enable us to grasp what he has experienced. It is not the chaos he is pursuing but the truth.

This is where we come in. We all are people of imagination. We constantly project images. We communicate in gestures and symbols. For that reason art has a profound bearing on all we do. Every person is a special kind of artist and is obliged to perfect his skill. And it is only within freedom that the skill proper to each of us can be perfected. We are all under pressure from others to project the "right" set of images, those which are conventional and accepted by a largely conservative people. This is something which must be resisted, irrespective of the resulting chaos, since what we project must be the truth as we see it and not a phony compromise. Within ourselves, and abstracting from any outer accomplishments, we all become great or shoddy works of art. Our life will be an expression of our place in the world and of its impact on us, or it will be meaningless. Through our art we cope with reality and build bridges to span the gaps that separate us from one another.

The hurt people of the world need those bridges. There are too many people living lives of "quiet desperation," tortured by family situations, by working conditions, by discrimination, by disrespect, by fears and guilt. They strike out at God, the Church, their fellow man because they have no credible symbol, image or art form presented to them that would make their life meaningful. They are scandalized by the uselessness of their own suffering. There is nothing heroic, romantic or praiseworthy about it. No one is going to pin a medal on them for having survived or endured. Who will be their artist and show them that it is the very passion of Christ, that they are the poor of God, the special ones? What image can you project that will reveal to them that they are the living icon of the living Christ?

There is no easy answer, at times no solution, for the many people in this state of chaos. The problem is too vast and too out of control. In the end there is faith, clear or confused—it doesn't matter much—in an understanding God or there is nothing at all. The religious leaders are busy; many are remote. Where will you find them when you need somebody to put his arm around your shoulder, uncover your very real beauty and be the artist you need? Perhaps there is only "Jesus Christ and him crucified." This may explain the proliferation of art works depicting the death of Christ. They make the reality of his trust, the dignity and nobility of his last hours, present to our chaos. Those who suffer will find Christ, not in the reflections of theologians and Scripture scholars but in the same bloody mess they are in themselves. They can recognize one of their kind who had nobody to help him, nobody to uncover beneath his failure the divine beauty that was his. But the mystics and the artists uncover it in some small way. They tell us that the Word, Christ, is spoken in each of us, that in the chaos of each tortured or fulfilled person the glory and art of Christ is visible to those who have eyes to see.

PRAYING THE PARADOX

My trouble with paradox began with my disliking doughnuts. It wasn't merely the degree to which the mouth had to be opened to accommodate them, nor the sickly sweet taste of them, nor the fullness of foam-rubber feeling in the stomach afterward, nor the residue of grease and powdered sugar that clung to the face from ear to ear. It was more subtle than that. The doughnut was Sister's work of art—which in itself was all right; everybody should have something one can do well. The problem was that if you did not sample the filthy things feelings would be hurt. Emotional blackmail entered the picture. When they were served at breakfast you could struggle through one of them with the required nods and smiles. But when they were served at dinner my back went up. Everything that Emily Post and the American way of life stood for was violated. Hurt feelings or not, one should not have to eat doughnuts at dinner.

I came to dinner famished, and there they were—a heaped tray full of them. It was a violation of one's sense of justice. I took a deep breath and decided that I would forego them. I picked up my food, moved to a table and sat hunched over my plate expecting the inevitable. The baker in question came with noisy enthusiasm and slammed down on a chair beside me. "I see you are not eating a doughnut," she said. "No," I replied. The response was abrupt. The expected reply was, "Oh, there are doughnuts, are there? I must get one." As it was, the direct assault caused a momentary setback. Following a pause to regroup she returned to the attack: "There's a tray of doughnut holes over to the side. You might like some of them." Now, this I found intriguing. I had never seen a tray of holes. There was something of mystery here that bore contemplating. I rose from the table and went over to the tray. But on seeing it I was disappointed. The holes were all incarnated—stubby sausage-like things which had come out from where the holes actually existed. But it got me thinking. I developed a whole new respect for the doughnut as the paradigm of paradox. Is the hole in the doughnut a "something" that actually exists, or is it a "nothing"? Is it something that is present or is it an absence? Is it, then, the presence of an absence? Let us remember that we are talking about the hole in itself. We are not talking about the dough. We must put aside the dough-nut and confine ourselves to the hole in itself, which is what is under discussion. Perhaps it cannot exist without the dough. On the other hand the doughnut cannot exist without the hole. If it had no hole, it would be an English muffin. This is amazing. Here is something, a doughnut, which is constituted in its very existence by a nothing, the hole. It relies for its very being on the presence of an absence. That approach to the lowly doughnut was very satisfying. Perhaps even we ourselves depend for our very existence and reality on the pres-ence of an absence—on the transcendent God. It is all very simple, of course: experience transcends reason; it does not follow the norms of law and order, and we have no adequate words to express it. This presence which is an absence, this something which is a nothing, was a paradox I had to bring to prayer. But in prayer we are not only dealing with the experience which transcends reason, we are dealing with the Mystery which transcends all experience. God cannot be adequately caught in any finite experience. It is altogether too much.

I sit with my back to a warm radiator. It is one of my favorite ways of prayer. I dislike being distracted by chills that fall from the windows when there's frost outside. The prayer begins in the usual manner: recalling that the Father has promised that he will grant in prayer whatever we ask in the name of Jesus. I ask that he grant me the gift of his Spirit that I may understand him and respond to him. I am quite aware that the enterprise is not commercial. I know from experience that God is not in the business of granting handouts which might boost my ego. Quite the contrary—one's vanity takes a beating if there is honesty in one's prayer. What I am seeking is a togetherness, a harmony with God in which I hope to come to know him, not merely something about him.

For a while nothing happens. It may even continue like this throughout the entire period. Should it do so it will not be time wasted. I try to enter God's presence but there is too much noise in my head. An image enters my mind: it's as if my head were the top part of a helicopter, its blades circling and slapping the air with a fearful noise. Beneath me I see the ocean at night. There is light reflected from it. The ocean is God. I want to separate myself from my head, let the blades drift off up and let myself drop down into the ocean. My head is not in harmony with my heart. "Pray with your head in your heart," the Fathers of the Church had advised. "Do not imitate, but interiorize Christ," they said. So I catch myself in time. It is a delightful illusion, a seduction really, to lose one's identity and be submerged in God, absorbed by the One. Whatever authentic experience I shall have of God, it must not destroy but rather establish my own personal reality. I brush the whole image away. Images are created; they are not God. They will be back, of course, but in the meantime I am looking for God as a person.

For a moment I am able to sit silent with God. Then in some quiet way I realize that he is present—not as an image, nor as insightful information. It is something more than that. He is present as an alive person. I experience him as the living God, not as a theological abstraction. It is himself that I know with an understanding that comes from togetherness. Or at least I know him by knowing one aspect of him, knowing him from one viewpoint, and from that viewpoint the God I know is a humble God. I experience the alive God and he is Absolute Humility. This is shocking. Of course, I tell myself, it had to be that way. I realize that I knew "about" him all along, but I did not know *him*. It is an awesome sight. I knew well that "he humbled himself (he made himself nothing) . . . he was more humble yet even to accepting death, death on a cross" (Phil. 2:7). But that was knowledge about him, whereas this is seeing it. In this absolute humility of his he has made himself less than I am. This is what is so awful. He has reversed our roles— as if I really could have a role relative to God. This is chaos out of hand. He defers to me. He is a servant God, a ministering God. This is not something he does for the moment. He is, in his essential being, the Absolutely Humble One, Absolute Humility. In view of this I am left sitting here with my ridiculous self-importance. It is not just enough that the humble God wishes to establish me in my own worth, but he chooses to be humble to accomplish it. The phony worth I think I have, and which I now see ludicrously reflected in his humility, is the worth of a complacent knothead. I realize that I am called to get down there and be more humble than absolute humility, and I know also that this is something impossible. It has nothing to do with groveling. It has to do with the acceptance of truth and my honesty in responding to it.

The simple fact of the matter is: I do not want a humble God, a God who in "emptying himself" has made himself less than I am. I want him up there where he is unreachable, where I can maintain my excuse for falling short of him. But here he is, alive, present, unavoidable and utterly humble. There can be no excuses. He has lowered himself and made himself completely approachable. In this ridiculous reversal of roles he lets me see that I am indeed a very poor substitute for God. He shows me that I have been playing at being a god in my own right. It humbles me, grinds into my innards. He shows me that it is much worse than that; I have been the anti-God, the clown god who did not even realize he was a clown. He has emptied himself to the point of being nothing, and he allows me to see that I am something. He does not comment on it. I am in the silence of God. It is sufficient to see the situation to realize how meaningless it is. And the offer is obvious: we may have our essential worth, and it is in him, if we too empty ourselves. Other than that, all worth is a poor joke.

What are we to do with a humble God? We cannot argue with him. Perhaps all we can do is allow him to establish us in that essential worth, in that humbling which is exalting, in the emptiness which is filled full. It is said that humility is truth. More accurately it is the recognition and acceptance of the finite truth about ourselves, or about anything. It would seem that God has nothing to be humble about within the Trinity. But even there the Father pours himself out infinitely into his Word of Truth, his recognition of himself, and accepts himself back in the infinite Spirit of love for that Truth. So, even there there is emptying, recognition and self-acceptance. But outside himself, or rather in what is other than himself, what God makes is finite. God cannot make another God or we would have two finite gods. There is something humbling about making a finite thing. One knows its limitations. And, strangely enough, the better made it is the more humble one feels about it precisely because of its limitations. God accepts the truth about what he has made, its goodness and its limitations. So there is no need to prove anything before God, especially not in prayer. Because he is Absolute Humility, absolutely secure in himself and in his self-emptying, he is able to accept us as his friends just as we are. We are served—nothing is imposed. He defers to our freedom. Everything is offered in gift, for all that every gift has a real purpose—one might almost call it a price tag—and the humility to which he calls us is not for nothing. We are put to shame by his humbleness, annihilated within ourselves because he has "emptied himself." We dare not turn anymore to observe ourselves, since doing so would be insufferable vanity in the face of God's humility. It is the paradox of God and our paradox that we have to give ourselves away to find ourselves, lose our life to save its real meaning, be an empty something, an absence that is the only true presence.

My mind is boggled. It is silent. What is there to say in this awesome silence before God and his humility? I cover my face with my hands, my body bends from the cushion on which I sit until my forehead touches the floor. I pause for a moment. Then the moment passes and I sit up again—but the humble God remains.

The mystery of it all—it is too vast: the beauty and brokenness of the world; the sublime that inspires us and the finite which hurts us; the Servant-God and the power in his powerlessness. What can give meaning to our lives? We go around in circles—around and around, up and down. Is it a mere merry-go-round, a carousel? Are we caught in life, unable to step off the whirligig, always returning to where we started years before? Our world is full of needy people and we, blinded by our own neediness, are unable to touch them. So we continue on up and down, around and around, with the music of the calliope a mockery in our ears.

Who are we, now that we pray, now that we stand empty and naked before God? Who are we when we are our true selves, when our pseudo-godliness is renounced? We wear a coat of many colors and we each wear a mask lest the world see our true face. We are a motley group indeed, "fools for Christ's sake," dressed in clowns' costumes—solemn and playful, aggressive and timid, brave and cowardly, helpful and indifferent, self-interested and unselfish, succeeding and failing, believing and still doubting, fearing and still hoping, achieving and still struggling. We are clowns tumbling in the ring, for Christ's sake: sad, or serious, or joyful clowns. The world closed in on itself has no meaning for us, but opened on God it is full of meaning. We are not the rich and powerful who save the poor. We are the poor who are saved, the humbled ones—prodigal son, woman taken in adultery, crucified thief, good Samaritan, tax collector. "Remember" (you humbled ones) "how generous the Lord Jesus was: he was rich, but he became poor for your sake, to make you rich out of his poverty" (2 Cor. 8:9). It is a paradox. Can we let you, Jesus, save us out of our poverty, heal our wounds, cover our shame, feed our hunger, forgive our sins, comfort our sorrow, fill our emptiness as we go up and down, around and around? Can we allow you that? Is it not sufficient merely to be ourselves since in your absolute humility you accept us as we are? Yet, when you come, when we hear the thunder in the distance, can we bow our heads? Can we just "be"?

When he comes our prayer will be light. There will be no further paradox. When he establishes his kingdom forever we shall acclaim him forever. When he appears surrounded by the heavenly host, when his glory is revealed, he will still be only who he is: the humble man walking to Calvary, struggling to carry his cross—a struggle now revealed in all its glory. When the carousel is still, when we have put off our clown's costume and are called to the center of the ring—"Come, blessed of my Father"—we shall still be only who we are, the people who went around and around, up and down. We shall be the people who struggled with our own Calvary, a struggle now revealed in its real glory.

Let us sit with this humble God. His humbleness sets us free. There are no barriers. The shock of his humility melts into happiness. It is altogether too chaotic. Rather, it is he who is happy and his happiness is communicable. "God is his own happiness"—it was St. Thomas Aquinas who said it. It is more than the fact that he is happy. It is more than even liking himself. He is, from within, the very source of his own happiness. Because he is Absolute Humility he is Absolute Happiness. His happiness does not depend on anything outside himself, on his great works of creation and salvation, on the fact that he is worshiped or loved. He does not have to look to rewards to make him happy. Nothing can diminish his joy. He is never displeased; if that were possible he would not be God and there would be little hope for a broken world. He is not subject to our limitations. He never tires of us or of our world. "I have told you this," he said, "that my own joy may be in you and your joy may be complete" (Jn. 15:11). We are called beyond the "doing" of God into his "being," into the "isness" of God. God *is* humility, he *is* happiness. A digression:

> There was a great king who had everything that money could buy. His kingdom was prosperous and at peace, but he was not happy. He called in his wise men and asked for a solution to his problem. Their conclusion was that just as he had received power through investiture, so also would he receive happiness. They searched the realm to find its happiest citizen. After a prolonged search they found him ... a blind beggar in a back alley. "Our king," they said, "is unhappy, and since you are the happiest man on earth we need to invest him in your cloak. In that way he too will become happy." "I am the king's loyal subject," said the beggar, "but a cloak I do not have. All I have is happiness."

In his humility, God surrenders all. He does it today as he did it yesterday. He shall do it forever. We stripped him of his cloak and clothed him in mockery. That truth, too, he accepted about himself and became for us the source of all joy. Our joy is never found in the cloaks of other people. God is himself the source of humble happiness within us, bringing about our joy through the medium of his presence. Yet his happiness is a gift no easier of acceptance than his humility. What shall we do with a happy God? How shall we accept the mystery of his being when he calls, "Enter into the joy of the Lord"? How shall we enter if not through his humbleness? But, then, his call brings about its own acceptance. We would not have recognized the call were we not already within his wordless presence.

My prayer is almost finished. For all my words, we spoke in silences. "I will be with you," he said. So, you will be with me, and time is passing. I pick God up (he made himself nothing) and tuck him under my arm—whatever—and begin again the long journey home. I go the long road home by the ocean, hearing again the slosh and slap of the waves among the rocks at Point Lobos. I sit by the Clearwater listening to the growling of the river and the splash of its whitewater as it cascades past. Neither thought nor thinking of mine will ever halt the water's flow. But there is frost on the fields and fog among the trees, and the yellow leaves of fall are splattered on the fog. I see nature, our mother, prowling around the fields, harvesting the ripe ones from their trees, and my heart is bursting with joy in the beauty of the world. Why, then, is it sad? Mother Nature, you seducer, you are not God, howsoever loudly you speak of him. Why must people, when most ripe, die? God, my God, it is not fair. It should not have to be. But it is the paradox of humility again that the saving is in the losing and the something is in the nothing, and that those who have the nothing possess all things. Let it be; my prayer is at an end. Amen to all paradoxes and to the chaos.

I kiss the floor before you because I am, of this earth, a part; of your making, finite. I uncross my legs and rise from my cushion. My knees are stiff and I stumble—but that is not my problem. My problem is, my God, that I shall never understand. You are too much. It is all too vast. The mystery is too great.

So, the heck with it, I'll make a pot of tea. Again, thank you, Lord. Amen.

CHAOS IN THE
HISTORY OF SPIRITUALITY

People come to you and say, "We never know what's going on in your mind. It bothers us." Your first reaction is to think, "How terrible that anyone should want to know what is going on in your head. Do people have a right to know what is in other people's heads?" Then your better nature struggles to the surface and you reply that it wasn't something you had thought of yourself. You suspect that it has something to do with their insecurity. If they could watch your mind the way they watch TV, they would be in control of the chaos. All those brooding, silent, ironic, abstract and unsightly thoughts leave everybody in a state of chaos. "A penny for your thoughts," they say. "What are you thinking about right now? You haven't been saying very much." "I was thinking that there are a hundred pounds of hamburger in a bull's neck." "Is that the kind of thinking you do? I thought that you were a spiritual person?" "Well, that's the whole point. It really is a very spiritual thought. Everything is spiritual." "I don't get it?" "It isn't possible to explain," you say, after taking a look inside your head. "It's a lot of bull, really," you laugh, and everybody is offended. Your head is full of wheels whirring and humming, buzzing with low fast sounds, and you have this understanding of all things happening at once, nothing happening in sequence, no before or after. To explain the matter you would have to put things in sequence. But you cannot do it since everything is one with God in his marvelous sense of rightness in the neck of a bull. And McDonald's is correct. It sells a lot of bull. God must be very pleased.

The next time you open the door of your skull and look inside, it is, perhaps, a vast empty space. All the wheels have packed up and gone. "I'm not thinking of anything at all." "But it isn't possible," they say; "you've got to be thinking of something. We never know what it is." You look for some small thing to offer and there is nothing—silence, almost complete; like a huge underground cavern, dark, with drops of water falling like single notes on a synthesizer, faint echoes of words but no words. It is all too vast for anything to be something. "Sorry, I'm not really thinking of anything; just being." But they have turned away to others and are not listening anymore. It is part of the chaos.

Tonight I saw a huge harvest moon—such things do still exist— rising to the east, coming up behind the Bitterroot Mountains, a deep blood orange: "The sun rose up at midnight,/ the sun rose red as blood;/ It showed the Reaper—the dead Christ/ upon his cross of wood." So what are we going to do about this spiritual life of ours? Cry for a hunger that cannot be satisfied, or laugh at the goodness of it all, or swear with frustration at the finite that chokes us, or be humble before the mystery of it all and conscious of our unworthiness? There are wheatfields between here and the Bitterroot, and they have already been reaped. Men are being harvested all over the world—women too. People are mourning and dying, praying and making love, working and just floating along. It is the spiritual life. And they want to know what is in other people's heads so that the chaos will not engulf them. A moment of silence shatters our noisy world and someone says: "What are you thinking?" And that someone is always disappointed that it amounts to so very little. But if your insight is great and you begin to tell such people of your struggle with mystery, they say, "Oh," and are embarrassed they spoke.

Would it be possible to begin at the beginning and keep it down to earth? Well, there was this man, Jesus. He turned out to be God, as the resurrection demonstrated for those who had faith to believe. He was, as Karl Rahner would put it, the "absolute bringer of salvation." He was, in himself, human salvation. And he gave his own Spirit to all those who are in his body, one Spirit given to all. What I am saying is that it is his doing. We do not get the Spirit from our own deep reflections or from our excited exclamations of religious enthusiasm. We get the Spirit because we belong to the body. There is no credit to us at all. So there is only one spiritual life, really, though there may be innumerable variations on the theme. The body, through word, work, sacrament and the aid of various organizers and public relations experts, mediates the salvific event, offers us the gift of the Spirit, confronts us with Christ. One basic spirituality.

There are two basic areas of chaos: our personal experience and our personal response. How we experience the Spirit varies from person to person as it is filtered through our unique humanness. But how we interpret what the Spirit is asking of us and respond to that asking also varies. The Spirit will remain the same but our understanding and response will vary. Marvelous chaos. Not just private, happy, silent, ironic and chuckling chaos either, but social as well. The mediation of Christ must be tailored and fitted to every age and culture. Here we have groups of them experiencing the Spirit, movements, whole nations. And it is not a doctrine or a concept but something happening, a way of life, as many spiritualities as there are individuals and groups. So we get a feel for the spiritual life as the very mystery of christian existence as it emerges from the presence and dynamic activity of the Spirit. We do not have to be pious or emotional about it. On the other hand, of course, should you be a colorful or eccentric personality your response may very well astonish your neighbors and still find a home within the Universal Thing.

To put it simply, the spiritual life is chaos for the mere reason that it is "life" and cannot be boxed in or defined. You do not sit God down in a rocking chair over against you and decide to have it out with him. Privately, socially or intellectually there is no way you can pin down the spiritual life in black and white. God will not fight, so there's no point in looking for explanations there. The thing has to be lived. We want to get it in control. We like to make a nice balance of things but the Spirit keeps irrupting from inside us with no respect at all for the nice balance we had made. For example: Arsenius, a Desert Father, late of the Emperor Theodosius' court, had a balance. Rome was bad for him. He fled to the desert with his mind made up never to look on the face of a woman again. It was too much for his psyche. Then a former lady friend of his came all the way from Rome to the desert to be edified. She was bothered and wanted to know what was in his mind. Furthermore, she wanted to look him in the eye as he told her. "Face to face," she said, and it was a command. He would not look up. She insisted. All she wanted, she said, was to be remembered by him. But he believed that for the mind to be free for contemplation all images and mental fantasies must be wiped away from it. "Look up," she said. So he looked up and prayed: "May God wipe the remembrance of your face from my mind." Whether God obliged or not we are not told, but the woman returned to Rome and fell ill because of the rejection. When she had been reassured by a local bishop that she was remembered in Arsenius' prayers, though not in his fantasies, she recovered. And then there was Paphnutius, known to everybody in the desert as "The Buffalo." He also was determined to keep his mind on God alone but he couldn't help being bothered because there were effeminate-looking men even in the wilderness. The trouble is this: we have our experience of the Spirit compelling us, but it is so garbled by our own personalities that we are not even sure, all of the time, if it is genuine or not. Then when we try to make a positive and reasonable response, one that is adequate and final, we find that there is nothing in our spiritual life that is "once and for all." Here they come again. This time there is a switch in the conversation: "Tell me," they say, "what is in my mind. Is my experience genuine? What is the valid response?" With all the wisdom that comes from making the mistake of answering such questions you try to respond by finding out what they think themselves. If the worse comes to the worst you show them that they are seeking law and order and certainty again. If the chaos can not be resolved at the moment, why not be happy with the chaos?

To resolve the problem, the Scriptures came up with the idea of discernment—the Jesuits too, only this time the Scriptures thought of it first. We have to "test the spirit to see if it be of God." Both experience and response have to be examined. There are the possibilities of angels of darkness masquerading as angels of light. To illustrate the point with another story from the Desert Fathers: An evil spirit appeared decked out in blinding light. He stood before one of the Fathers and said, "I'm the angel Gabriel and I have been sent to you." The old man looked up at the dazzling figure and said: "Somebody made a mistake. You've got the wrong man." With that humility the demon was banished. Why? Because humility discerns. But it is not always that simple.

People get to worrying about others who have a noticeable measure of the Spirit. "What's got into her?" "What is back of this movement?" Who is empowered to discern? Ultimately, only the body which received the spirit in the first place has the power to discern the spirit. To set oneself up as having one's own private enterprise with God, and apart from the body—no longer needing it—is sheer farce. Not that the more important people in the body are not pretty heavy-handed at times, forgetting that though they are discerners they also need discerning. There is a story to illustrate the point: There was this synod of whales and they brought in a little shrimp who had been making unwelcome sounds. They decreed that he should be thrown out of the ocean. Then another little shrimp got up nervously and said, "I, too, sound off and will leave the ocean with him." At this, the whole assembly was put to shame because everybody knew that when whales sounded off there were tidal waves. Discernment tests sincerity. It explores all the pros and cons in the chaos so that a choice may be made. Is the idea theologically sound? Is the response unselfish? Does this course of action benefit the people of God? Is this self-exaltation or surrender? Is it a constructive or a destructive force? With the aid of prayer and dialogue we look into the chaos and arrive at a decision. It does not have to be the best of all possible decisions, but no matter—God will grace sincerity.

For centuries martyrdom was looked upon as the great discerner. It unequivocally proved a point, the total surrender of the martyr to God. It was looked upon as the most sincere expression of the spiritual life. It had to be death for love of God and his truth, not merely a political killing. For years no other expression of the spiritual life was deemed conclusive of holiness. But we do not have to go that far, or, if you wish, the opportunities for martyrdom are not offered to all of us. But the Gospel, quite calmly and without apology or compromise, demands quite a detached attitude to life. The spiritual life does not allow us to play games and have the best of two worlds. It is not a question of rejecting an evil world. It is more a question of not being absorbed by the good things in a very good world. One must go beyond it. Wherever the experience of the Spirit has been genuine, people have always transcended their own and this world's interests. Their narrow human limitations have opened out on the infinite, defying logic and reason. We may be puzzled by the manner of their response but we cannot doubt their sincerity. St. Simon got up on a fifty-foot pillar for the rest of his days—it was the best, he felt, he could do to express his love for God—and they called him "the Stylite." It had nothing to do with his having a certain style or flair. Others got into the palm trees in the desert oases and refused to come down. They called them Dendrites. Still others continued to have their heads severed. They accepted it willingly, if fearfully, refusing to stand on their rights. Rights, dignity and reverence for your person have had little to do with the spiritual life. Chaos, the head being pulled in two directions, is a place for choice. It is a good thing to protect one's life. For a reason, it is a good thing to lose it. Some opted to let the head go. The lawyers had no advice to offer even though the kingdom of heaven was offered to the generous. It was strictly a matter of choice, an offer of freedom, a gift of the Spirit. You might lose your head, there being faith and no logic in the thing, and gain a crown with no head on which to place it. Even in its metaphors the Church is paradoxical.

It would be a great mistake to think that in the great age of the martyrs people lined up to experience "the short, sharp, shock." (I am not being flippant. The martyrs died because they knew that life was a celebration, not because they were full of lugubrious solemnity.) Most of the Christians lined up to throw incense on the fire as a sign of emperor-worship. There were so many of them in the North African church that they had to be turned away each evening and asked to return in the morning. Others bought the "papers" that proved they had worshiped, thus becoming the Church's first casuists. In spite of the thousands who were beheaded, crucified, thrown to the beasts and burned alive there were thousands of others who chose to save their skins. They became part of the chaos. The Church of the day was not quite informed as to whether it could, or could not, absolve those who had apostatized. Within its own chaos the Church itself had to come to self-awareness. It had to discover, by studying the human condition of its members, what the extent and possibilities of its saving mission really were. After observation, prayer and discussion—its own form of discernment—it concluded that, in fact, there was no sin that could not be forgiven provided that the sinner was truly repentant.

The heroism of the few is always needed. It shows us the experience of the Spirit and the response in an absolute way. It proves that a total surrender of one's life to God is possible. But the over-all holiness of this body of Christ of ours is found in the daily humdrum fidelities, repentances, prayers and struggles of its sinful members. This leads us to see that abandoning the body because its members are sinful is utterly fraudulent. A pious friend of mine once said to me, "How disappointed God must be that the clergy are not more holy." I replied, "You would have to admit, then, that God has failed in our regard. Perhaps he never expected us to be any better." He gave me a very queer look. To have failed and to have been forgiven is the lot of the vast majority of people. It is a seeming mediocrity only from a pious point of view. Heaven is made up of forgiven people and there is no mediocrity there. There are no misfits in heaven, which leads us to believe that in the overview of God there are fewer misfits than we might think on earth. The Spirit is at work in the chaos so that he might be the guiding power in the decisions that come from it, decisions of individuals and of the Church. And the work of the Spirit continues on even when the Church leaders are timid or cannot agree.

The age of the Desert Fathers and the beginnings of monasticism followed the age of persecutions. But the chaos continued. Flight to the desert did not solve everything, but it had its great moments. There is a story from the desert which is uncomfortably modern in its tone: A couple of chauvinistic young men entered the desert in pursuit of holiness. There wasn't anything much happening there and the days got a bit tedious. They heard of the great Mother Sara, and how holy a woman she was. It irked them and they decided to put her humility to the test. "Let us go and bring this heifer down," the one said to the other. On their arrival they said to her, "Are you not proud that the men of the desert come to visit you, a woman?" She took one look at them and snorted: "It is I who am the man in this desert and you are a pair of sissys."

Those were great days in the life of the Spirit, and they laid the foundation for all the spirituality that followed. For all their mistakes, they wanted radical and pure Christianity. It was not all a matter of physical asceticism. There was simplicity of life-style, hospitality to no-account travelers who came by for a "touch," quieting of the passions, gentleness, forgiveness, work, prayer without ceasing (Since you can, Lord/ and since you know, Lord,/ Lord have mercy), having a pure intention in all they did, discretion—the knack of knowing the loving thing to do, controlling the thoughts and humor. Thousands flocked to the Egyptian and Syrian deserts. In Egypt they were mostly the *fellahin,* the poor farmers who were unable to pay the exorbitant taxes of the Roman conquerers, but there were also educators, clerics, politicians and an occasional robber escaping from justice. There were Pythagoreans, Origenists, Neo-Platonists, and Arians as well as the more orthodox. Some of them stayed in their cells and became wise from thinking and prayer. Some served others and became wise from serving. Some wandered in mind as well as body and wound up in the brothels of Alexandria or brawling about theology in the city squares. Could we even begin to imagine the possibility of a riot in one of our city squares today over a point of theology? The Spirit is shackled because we have too much control on the chaos. Our celebrations of "the freedom of the children of God" are so genteel. Ah well . . . the moon is silver in the sky now, and glistening on the water through the pine trees. The beauty of it. But the water is merely a large cesspool. Does it matter . . . really? Had I not told you, you would not have known. The All-Holy shines on our human condition even when it is less than pleasing, and it is beautiful.

The desert, like all our chaotic deserts, was reeling and staggering with hungry men drunk with the Spirit. Serapion sold the only book he had, a copy of the Gospels, and said: "I have sold the book which taught me to sell all and give to the poor." Brother Lot came to Abba Joseph for advice. Now the trouble with Brother Lot was that he had become a little complacent about this spiritual life thing. With some affection he said to Abba Joseph: "I keep my little fast. I do my little meditation. I strive to empty my thoughts. What more should I do?" Abba Joseph lumbered to his feet, like a huge bear waking up, and raised his hands to heaven. His ten fingers became ten blinding lights. "Why not be completely turned into fire?" he replied, looking down at Brother Lot with disarming simplicity. And along those same lines there is a story about a brother who always doubted himself. He came to an old monk who had a reputation for insight. "What do you think, Father?" he said. "How do I look to you?" "You look like Jesus Christ to me," said the old man. "Go back and continue doing what it is you do." The brother went away very much comforted, but a few days later he got to worrying again. He returned to the Father and said: "What do you think now, Father? How do I look to you?" "You look like the devil to me," said the Father. "You talk too much." Another man came searching for God in the desert, but did not know what to do with his daughter. He disguised her as a boy and brought her into the monastery with him. Time passed and the man died. But his daughtter, Maryana, stayed on, her sex unknown. Some time later a local girl got pregnant and Maryana was accused of the fatherhood. She was cast out of the monastery to do penance. She persevered in the penance and was readmitted four years later. It was not until her death that anybody knew she was a woman. Caesar of Heisterbach has a like story about the daughter of a dead Crusader who disguised herself and entered a Cistercian abbey. Legends, if you wish. The point is that there was something in the desert that inspired legends. The stories reveal a feeling people have that somehow or other they must transcend themselves to be themselves. They also tell us that it is perfectly all right for people to have to search, to make outrageous mistakes and be overwhelmed by the chaos in spiritual affairs. They tell us that now, as well as then, there are no finalized norms of response to the Spirit. One has choices and decisions. There will be mistakes, all the more surely since what Christ offered us was a new life, not a code of ethical behavior.

The chaos will continue. But it might be well to consider some of the more obvious ways in which our response to the Spirit may be mistaken. Among them we have:

Enthusiasm: turning the experience of the Spirit into extraordinary reactions. The gift of tongues is over evaluated. People look for visions, pseudo-miracles, ecstasy. There is an attempt to make the Spirit one's private possession. There is a curiosity for the extraordinary, a sort of lust to see and experience over and above belief.

Institutionalization: Here, every expression of the Spirit is turned into a solidified institution in which the gift of the Spirit begins to be equated with the institution itself. The purpose of the institute, which was to preserve the gift and make it available to all, is distorted into excluding all but the few. A woman with a gift of healing founds, often without intending to, a religious institution to continue her work. It winds up being a huge business enterprise with few, if any, of the institute's members working in it. A man has an insight into a mystery of Christ. Others join him, inspired by the dynamism of it. Some organizer draws up rules of behavior and the congregation begins to have "clout" at the political level. The final stage arrives when the rule is equated with the group's spirituality.

Rationalization: Here the spiritual life is understood as a philosophical or intellectual movement, a dematerialized spirituality. Devout people come together and discuss their principles and values. Their idealistic values may have no relationship whatever to their life-style.

Irrational Movements and Cults: These are usually combined with an anti-intellectualism, a refusal of serious study and scholarship. They may be founded by individuals who have certain psychic powers or powers to dominate others. The movement may result in mere pietistic exaggerations or it may became a very destructive cult. They are self-serving movements which oftentimes had very unselfish beginnings.

Dualism: This is a body/spirit split. The body is held in disregard. The unity of the person is forgotten. So also is the holiness that the incarnation conferred on matter.

Sentimentality: This continues to be a problem even in the present. It is reflected in much of our church ornamentation. Here, people give themselves over to emotional devotions devoid of all theological foundation.

When we look for something genuine in the chaos of our experience and response we find it in an unselfish love which creates unity, but not uniformity. False spiritualities separate people. One tires of people in the active ministry who belittle the life of cloistered religious. The more active a person will be for Christ, the more will that person appreciate the purpose of the cloister. One gets equally tired of the pious paternalism of some cloistered people who speak as if they had a lobbying power with God denied to all others—the "powerhouse of prayer" syndrome. One would expect them to be as well informed on what is happening in local religious education as they are on global matters. There are other examples of the unity/disunity chaos. Celibates are in a poor position to lecture the married on their responsibilities. The married should hesitate to lecture the sisters on their life-style since they cannot know what is in a sister's head, and it should not bother them. There is no status, no competition among those who are genuinely moved by God's Spirit. A union with God that implied separation from others, or any condemnation of others, or disinterest in sinners, or superiority of any kind is the very opposite of the Christian spiritual life. We are all profitless servants; we have only done what was expected of us and what we have has been given us in gift.

But unity is not uniformity. This protects the element of freedom in the chaos. What the norm of behavior is for one is utter nonsense, even grotesque, for another. The person of the Spirit will be understanding of the eccentricities, extravagances and even the occasional violence of people who are trying to respond to the Spirit's presence. The experience and the response are filtered through broken human personalities. The gift of the Spirit will express itself differently in the sanguine, melancholic, mousy, intellectual and psychotic temperaments. And in the sight of God, who is to say which is the more holy? We shall not be judged by our accomplishments but by how we accepted the grace that was offered to us and how we responded to God's gift of himself. There will be surprises "when the saints come marching in." What to do, then? St. Augustine would advise us to love unselfishly and do whatever we feel called upon to do. We can respond freely and creatively only to our own unique experience.

Have you experienced God? That question on the lips of emotional people can be terribly annoying. The implications are obvious: If you have not experienced him, you jolly-well better be converted. Hidden in the question is the notion that God is an isolated object, someone you might run into down the street. There is also a real, if subtle, implication that we are on a par with God. God is God and we are we in our relationship with him. We supposedly can face him down with an empirical, objectified experience. We speak as if we might discuss the running of the world with him and suggest some well-needed improvements he may be overlooking. He is, of course, considered to be of more importance than Pope or president, but since he says so much less than both, one is tempted to take liberties. So, have you had your experience of God today? In Cambodia the crucial question is: Have you had your rice today? Do you realize what the petition is: "Give us this day our daily bread"? And we should know that it is in the bread and the rice and in all that we need to be fully human that our experience of God is found.

In the first place, every experience we have is had in our humanness. It is a human experience. We are not capable of a divine experience simply because we are not divine. We cannot hear, see, touch, taste or smell the Spirit of God. People are not wanting who would be willing to say that they at least smelled spirit: fragrances for saints, sulphur with a smidgeon of garlic for the devil. Granted, the range of human experience is vast and, at its highest levels, subtle. But the incarnation of God made it final, and terribly clear, that the experience of God at its fullest is the very human flesh and blood of Christ. What is seen is very human, and we who see it see God. "Something which has existed from the beginning, that we have heard, and we have seen with our own eyes, that we have watched and touched with our hands—this is our subject" (1 Jn. 1:1). God who is risen into us is revealed and experienced today in living signs, the people who do his will.

In the second place, God is infinite and we are finite. Every experience we have is a finite experience. But whatever human experience faces us up to, and opens us out to the infinite is an experience of God. Whenever we are moved beyond ourselves in moments of awe, praise, thanksgiving or forgiveness we experience God. All unselfish love faces us up to God, no matter how human may be its circumstances, no matter how far God may have been from our conscious thoughts at that moment. There is only one love and it is always divine. Only the caricatures are human. To love unselfishly is an experience of God because it transcends the human-enclosed-on-itself. It has nothing to do with sentiment, feeling or exaltation. It is God welling up within us, not God "out there." Whenever we did a good deed without thought of recompense, whenever we granted full forgiveness, whenever we reached out in caring and sharing without thought of receiving gratitude, and whenever we brought some small moment of freedom into the life of another, God was in the experience. God is experienced in whatever and whoever has no purpose in being except to be set aside as sacred to him. The experience of God is always found in our human experience even when it is the highest form of ecstasy. He is never an object, like a bag of spuds, out there. No matter how dark our life in the Spirit may be, no matter how hopeless or chaotic our inner feelings are, we can always touch God in simple and unselfish deeds to others.

The divine we see in Christ is that absolute sacredness to the Father that is revealed in his total surrender to him. It is his infinite self-transcendence, his absolute love. Truly this is the Son of God and we who see him see the Father. The experience of God is not some incredible set of coincidences, some mind-blowing exaltation; it is not an ecstasy or a vision but something within the grasp of all. What put it within the grasp of all was the entry into God of our humanness in the person of Christ. It is a simple moment within the chaos of human affairs when we choose to transcend our selfishness. "Out there" and "in there" have nothing to do with it. He is not localized. He is experienced in our setting ourselves and others free.

It is the individual who is important. Only individuals are canonized. Groups are not unless it is clear that each member of the group was a martyr. Movements seem to have a spiritual life of their own, but it is only the collected spiritualities of people who have banded together. This is true even when the movement has swept some very vocal riffraff into it. The movement carries those who need support and becomes a symbol of the Church at large. Nor can any movement guarantee that it will come up with a great leader. The refusal to accept the leaders we have on the grounds that we need or deserve greater or better is a common temptation. We always need and deserve better. The Spirit of God works mightily through outstanding leaders, but also works quite effectively without them. It was not to the great leaders of his day that Christ turned but to twelve rather backward men whom he made his apostles. It is part of the chaos. All the Spirit needs is sincerity.

Part of the problem for the individual is that it is not always easy to maintain one's sincerity, to avoid extremes, to avoid taking one's wishes for reality. Our spiritual life should not be so serious that it can afford to be touchy, nor so giddy that it is vain. It is not a ceremonial stage show in which religiously-minded people are on display. Neither is it fun and games. It takes a sense of humor to enable us to cope with the chaos of it all. People are coming from various frames of reference in their experience of study, inner freedom, attitudes to life, culture and grace of God. The Spirit adds to the chaos because he insists on "blowing where he will, no one knowing where he comes from or whither he goes." Nor is he subject to our law and order. But he brings unity to those who love and forgive even when he never tries to make them think or act alike.

The orders, congregations and societies all responded in their own unique way to the Spirit. The married and the single and the secular institutes all have their own valid and dynamic spiritualities. There never could be only one response, a better or a worse way. There is only the powerful irruption of the Spirit of Christ, ever active and impelling, within our Church and world. All who are in Christ, even those who are not aware of it, accept his Spirit. By their fruits they are known. All that God wants of us is to take the risk of doing something as a response to his presence whatever the chaos. The spiritual life is not determined by measurable results but by the freedom of the children of God that the Spirit offers us.

In the End
THERE IS CHAOS

"Why did he have to die?" "Why me?" It is the chaos. There actually is no reason why he or why you or why anybody. Nowhere in life is the chaos more evident than in taking leave of life. Dying is not subject to law and order. It is out of our control. It is reality—accept it or reject it as you may—and reality is chaotic.

That our span of life should draw to a close is perfectly natural. It is the inevitable consequence of our humanness. Were we not to die it might be difficult to say what manner of creature we would be, but we would not be human as we know it. Death is as much an integral part of our human condition as living. We eat and drink, we work and pray, we laugh and then we die. How long we shall live and when we shall die are altogether uncertain. They are purely contingent, and therefore within the realm of chaos. They are not subject to laws of behavior. It is wholly uncertain and unpredictable when death shall find us. Let us face this reality: there is absolutely no promise made anywhere, no guarantee, no right that we should live five years, twenty-five, or ninety-five. We may act with prudence and perhaps extend our life, but death at any age is an event to be expected and utterly out of our control. Irrespective of any outer or inner force, to say nothing of prudence, we die because we are human. For that reason, we can never ask with any real conviction, "Why me?" The sad fact is, "Why *not* you?" We can never say with any final logic or any "rights of the case" that another should not have died. It did happen. There were no guarantees that it would not

73

happen. That happening is the only reality. That it happened simply showed that of thousands of possible times this was the person's time. It could have been the day before or the following year. There is no plan. It happens when it happens. That is all—utter chaos and no norm to control it. We have no "right" to a ripe old age, and we have no right "not to die." There really is no time for the happening. That is chaos for our orderly minds. The next big question is: "Why did God not do something? We prayed and he did not answer our prayers." First of all, he did not do something because this world is its own world and we are free to be our own selves. If God started interfering we would be puppets. And every prayer has to be answered but in the manner that he sees fit, not according to our specifications. In the end the prayer that did not seem to be answered will be crucial for everything. It is the loss of God, not the loss of life, that is tragic.

It would be an ideal situation if the time of our dying were experienced as a time of preparation, of great spiritual activity. It would be good to be able to approach death consciously, with great dignity, preparing ourselves to experience this great mystery with inner freedom and surrender. We can even long for that ideal. Our end being as sacred as our beginning, we should desire that nothing be done to stunt it. But the real-life situation is oftentimes far from this ideal. It is part of the chaos. Death often comes without warning or time for preparation. It is, perhaps, resented, or is the object of rebellion. Cut off in the middle of life and of one's life-work, one senses that death is meaningless. So people worry about the death of one who never had a chance to experience life, or who never came to grips with life and its problems, whose development was left unfinished. What can we say? That life is cruel, or that God is cruel? That somebody is to blame? Or do we have the freedom to risk saying that such chaos is a part of the human condition, and that nobody is to blame? It is because God made us to be so free, so totally our own person, that so much chaos happens to us. Anything else would make us less than the persons we are destined to be. We could point to Christ and say that the death of God's own Son had all the elements of chaos. Cut off in the middle of life, his work in a shambles, rejected, betrayed, uncomforted, he accepted the will of his Father. "Why have you rejected me?" Why indeed? Even Jesus could not answer that one. His own death is our answer. It gives us hope. In this senseless death of Christ there is a real message that in

the eyes of God an untimely death is of no less value than the death
of the elderly who fade out in peace. What it says is this: God alone
is the Lord of life and death, and his power, not our efforts, gives
meaning to every person's death, chaotic or not.

For Old Testament man nothing was more precious than life:
"All that a man has he will give for his life" (Job 2:4). Life is God's
gift, the highest good. A full life is celebrated in the company of
others in security, peace, happiness and health. It was limited in
time, of course, but then God stood at the end of it just as he had
stood at its beginning, and that end could be approached as a
fulfillment and without fear. One could die peacefully, trusting in
God. This was the ideal realized in Abraham. He had received a
promise: "You shall go to your fathers in peace; you shall be buried
in a good old age" (Gen. 15:15). Years passed, we are told, and
"Abraham breathed his last and died in a good old age, an old man
and full of years" (Gen. 25:18). Scripture shows us that this is indeed
a blessing from God, and it would be good to experience one's dying
in this way. But then, as now, it was seldom that such an ideal was
realized.

Even now the number of those who die of old age is limited.
There has always been a dark chaotic side to dying. Scripture
frequently reveals this side of the mystery also. Since God was so
clearly seen as the God of life, dying could not but be looked upon by
many as anything other than a curse from God. The dying man was
oftentimes shunned by family and friends lest they also incur the
curse. There was some good reason in this since they did not
understand the mystery of contagion. But the dying man laments in
the psalms and elsewhere that he has been forgotten by God. He
gives way to loneliness and bitterness. Why, if God promised life, did
he permit death? It was in this light that St. Paul saw death. He tried
to grapple with the chaos of it. Death, for Paul, reveals who people
are under the power of sin. Since there is death there must have been
sin somewhere, because death is nothing other than the bitterness of
being abandoned to ourselves. This, strangely enough, is the death
experienced by Christ. As Paul saw it, he "became sin" nailed to the
cross. For "cursed is he who hangs on the tree." That was the Old
Testament man's understanding of death and, consequently, the
understanding of Jesus. In his rejection he experienced the weight of

the world's sin. What was salvific was that throughout all of this he never stopped trusting in the Father, nor stopped loving those who were killing him. It is this that gives meaning to any person's death, whether peaceful at the end of a long life or seemingly unfair and lonely. We so live, in Christ, that we may go through our dying trusting in the Father who alone gives it meaning.

What matters is the orientation of the whole of our life toward death. A young person can die with every bit as much understanding and fortitude as an elderly person. In the end, dying is not unnatural but natural. We have a purpose in what we do. It is the purpose which makes things meaningful. The purpose in a young person's life may be very deeply felt by that person, even if he or she may not be able to put words on it. Life is lived so that at the end there might be fulfillment. It is natural to expect fulfillment. Only a world enclosed on itself feels that life is its own fulfillment and that nothing follows. What follows is the fullness and transformation of that life as the inheritance one achieved. Death reveals fully, and for the first time, who one really is. No job, no accomplishment, no social status—not even that of president or Pope—can reveal who a person really is. Death reveals the achieved destiny of one whose life was oriented to fulfillment beyond this life.

We have no advance knowledge as to what the nature and circumstances of our dying shall be. There are no norms, laws or procedures which might put it within our control. We have a choice, however, in regard to death as we have in all the other forms of chaos in our life. The choice is so to live that our death will not be a final confirmation of our isolation from others. When dying is seen this way by the person who has a love for life, the shadow of death does not take anything away from the greenness of the grass, the singing of the birds, the laughter of children, the joy of love, or the strength of the trust which is embedded in one's faith.

When we are faced with the dying process of one we love, we are faced with mystery and with some element of inner chaos. What do we say? There are no simple topics. Now if the person were going to Hawaii there would be no problem. There would be lots to discuss. But, faced with dying, the usual conventions of interacting, the rituals of our behavior toward each other, do not work anymore. We search within our inner chaos for something to say or do. We try to cope with the totally unknown, and many of our words and body-language messages are frightfully childish: (a) "He brought it on himself. He never took care of himself." (b) "Think of how many people are worse off than you"—as if that were a help. (c) "Well, we must all go some day"—at best an attempt to make what is mystery reasonable; at worst, that dying is a matter of indifference. Meanwhile the help that is offered is oftentimes childish: (a) Hopelessness—"It's too bad you are ill. I'm really sorry." (b) Mild rejection or an unwillingness to be emotionally involved—"You have to carry your cross, you know." (c) Insincerity (the worst of all)—"You'll be out of here in no time. You're looking much better today." The trouble is that the dying usually know that they are dying. They have their own chaos multiplied by the conspiracy of silence in which nobody will speak the truth. They are forcibly drawn into playing the charade, and it is a humiliation for them to be part of an untruth.

We have to have a faith approach, a spirituality which offers people the encouragement to die in the power of Christ's Spirit. We should not hesitate to strengthen people who are ill with the promise of a future greater life, a higher level of personal existence which "eye has not seen nor ear heard," so great is its magnificence. The dying person should be made to feel that he is not alone, that the death of one has meaning for all. One's dying may seem to have little impact on anybody. The superficial talk continues, the plans for next week, the noise of the healthy. Yet dying is the most meaningful act of any person's life. Any dying person may lay down his life for others, which is the most significant thing anyone can do in a whole lifetime.

That world for which Christ does not pray (Jn. 17:19), the world sufficient to itself, whose end is itself, does not support dying. Dying is a mockery of the salvific power of politics, economics and knowledge. It disrupts the whole order of things, disturbs the balance. That some people, be they saints or fanatics, have no fear of surrendering their lives is a complete anomaly to a society that is its own savior. Society cultivates youth, the accumulation of wealth, the stockpiling of weapons and the false optimism that a paradise is just around the corner if other nations would only see things the way we do. The chaos of dying challenges the world's myth. The elderly become a part of the economic problem. The world, in fear for its existence, has nothing to offer the dying. Nothing challenges the invincibility of its values so much as someone up and dying. It is not to be examined too closely. It does not have a place in TV commercials.

Society conspires with itself to hide this ultimate chaos. Changes have taken place in recent decades to shield us from the impasse. The life-span of people in this country has been extended to the point where children are grown to adults before they experience the dying of their parents. This means that death was not part of their life experience at a time when they were forming their concept of reality. When it is encountered later it, of necessity, appears as something unreal, a situation of chaos. Parents frequently live at a distance from their children, with the result that their decline is not witnessed. In the past the dying process took place in the home, but now hospitals shield us from observing it and having to cope with it. Doctors and nurses play a professional role, protecting relatives from any personal care for the dying person, and protecting themselves from any emotional involvement. Morticians prepare the body which in an earlier age was laid out at home. They notify the newspapers and contact the clergy. Lawyers take care of the questions of property. Society makes sure that we are involved as little as possible. A business and industrial world makes no provision for mourning: "Smile, the customer expects it." Put together, all these factors contribute to making the mystery of dying and death more distant and unreal. They add to the helplessness of those who are mourning and isolate them from any meaningful involvement. Indirectly, they contribute to the isolation of the dying person, implying that he or she is a burden on people and in the way. The grief of loss is more difficult to integrate into our lives.

There are some things we might do to enable us to work our way through the chaos of dying. One would be to visit the sick more frequently, and with an attitude of sincerity, honesty and openness. The dying instinctively recognize sincerity. It is sufficient to be there, to be loving and to wait. All the dying person wants is that somebody be there and care. Given time, the sick person will share, or ask a question, or confide if there is something on his mind. Just saying it lifts a great burden off the mind of the terminally ill person. One does not have to have any advice to offer. It is sufficient to say that we understand, and that God understands.

But apart from ministry to the dying, we should develop a

prayer form which could enable us to keep in touch with our mortality. It would be a rehearsal of our own death. Well, why not? We rehearse for everything else that is important in our lives, and the coming "moment of truth" is absolutely unavoidable. The purpose of the prayer would be that such a reality be understood upon arrival, that a method of coping with it be developed long in advance. It might take the following steps:

1. Sit down and spend some time reviewing the positive elements in your life from childhood to the present. These positive elements form who you really are. The negative elements are empty spaces; say you are sorry for them and drop them.

2. Disengage yourself within your mind from family, friends and the good earth. Say goodbye to each of them. It may be an emotional moment. Let it be. Move on now. Disengage yourself from time and space.

3. Separate yourself from your subliminal depths. Let go of all angers, bitterness, anxieties and all worries about the futures of others. Enter the peace and powerlessness of the experience with total trust in God. Look at God. Avoid the vanity of thinking there is reason to fear him.

4. Be aware of being one with the whole body of Christ, head and members, and of being lifted up on their prayers to the Father. Rest in the prayer of the universal Church.

5. Enter into the presence of the infinity and intensity of God's love for you. Surrender. Let God's love reveal to you who you really are. It will be a judgment on you.

6. Give yourself in Christ to the Father and to the presence of all those who have gone before you.

In the face of death all escapes are an evasion. We must face reality. Some have felt that death has made the whole of life an absurdity, an abandonment to chaos, a fall into nothingness. Others ignore it and keep busy so as not to have to think about it. Still others decide that they will think about it when it happens—not a terribly intelligent approach to what will be the most decisive moment of their whole life. But death is always present in life, no matter how cleverly we try to hide from it. It colors very much of what we do, from taking out insurance policies to the food we eat. For people of faith it is a religious event. On his way to be thrown to the beasts St. Ignatius of Antioch could write: "It is a beautiful thing for me to die in Christ Jesus." The faith approach to this ever-chaotic event is quite valid. It allows us to see it as an open door to a higher form of personal living. It gives us hope. Confronted with death, we are called upon to investigate eternity, to evaluate our lives and to orient them in the light of that eternity. There is no great difficulty here, because eternity is not a task to be accomplished but a gift to be received.

To die with dignity implies that we have lived with dignity. We choose to live a full life. When death comes we must choose to die. We cannot look to society to help us with this choice. It has never accepted death as something meaningful. Society is confronted with its own problem: Is society permanent and immortal, and are individuals mortal and passing away? Now that we have nuclear weapons and the possibility of the total destruction of life, society itself appears threatened. Society says that it knows nothing of the dead. They are of no concern. And so it goes on to present us with a purely functional and scientific view of life. Its propaganda tells us that all that exists is what can be experienced by the senses. In this way it robs life of its true meaning, a meaning that can be discovered only in a dialogue with inevitable and unavoidable death. The meaning of life is discovered when we are conscious of death.

The single greatest discovery in the history of human existence, a discovery that brought unbelievable chaos, was the insight: "We die." It is not death itself but our consciousness of death that structures the whole of our life. The whole of human civilization emerged from that original insight. Humans alone are conscious of approaching death; animals do not know of it. Imagine a time before humans arrived at a point of self-consciousness, before they lost their innocence to self-awareness. They knew nothing of death. There was only the experience of the moment. There was no awareness of any need to provide for the future. Like the birds of the air and the lilies of the field they had no need to be concerned. They did not "spin or reap or gather into barns." It was, in a way, a sort of paradise. There were no "rights" to protect. Life was harsh but there was no concept "harshness" and no worry about what the future would bring. With the gradual emergence of self-consciousness all that changed, and there came the awareness of vulnerability. One day—there had to be a first time—in the presence of what they had seen time and time again but never pondered, there came the stunning insight: "I, too, shall die." It was horrendous knowledge. With it came the need to protect oneself against death. With the need came the "right." We are entitled to protect ourselves against what threatens our life. Rights clash and chaos breaks in on their consciousness. Norms would be drawn up to establish the rights and regulate them. From now on all the functions of living, working, hunting, controlling territory, eating and fighting would be done in conscious awareness of the possibility of death. Laws would be written, tribes formed, weapons perfected, cities founded and nations marked out so that we could most effectively protect ourselves against the common enemy, death. Civilization was born. People began to grab for power and possessions. Even the Bible has the descendants of Cain, the murderer, the ones who fashioned the laws and built the cities. Following the insight, there was another possibility, of course, but a slim one. In the awareness of another's right to life our forefathers might have been willing, out of love, to forego their own right and accept vulnerability to death. This they chose not to do, so sin, essentially "protecting ourselves against death," entered the world.

There is no question of saying here that it would have been better if we had stayed in a state of un-self-consciousness. It was out of the chaos of knowing that we shall die, and the consequent need to protect ourselves, that all human growth emerged. And given the background out of which we came and are still coming, a background of millenniums in which there were no rights, it is hardly likely that with the arrival of intelligence we should also have arrived at immediate heroic love for the neighboring caveman. All that Scripture says about our beginning is that it is attributable to God, but that sin and evil are our own doing. They are the product of our self-protecting, self-indulgent choices. To protect ourselves against death at the expense of others was a poor, even if inevitable, choice. How could we have known in those primitive days that death was the gateway to life? Now that we know, we are hardly less primitive.

The purpose in the development of civilization was that one day we would accept God's gift of himself. In the fullness of time, we being ready for the great revelation as to what life was all about, God came in the person of Jesus of Nazareth. He took upon himself our death and thereby transformed its meaning. It is no longer utter destruction but an open door back to our Creator. He showed us that it was no longer necessary to fear death, and therefore it was no longer necessary to protect ourselves against it. We could lay down our lives even for our enemies. He commanded us to love them. It is a magnificently freeing revelation, but the option to cease protecting ourselves is very difficult.

I suppose it is a bit disappointing, in a way, but Jesus did not have any program for the "good life." On the contrary, and it may appear morbid but it is not, he taught us how to die. He taught us that to love everybody, even those who killed us, and to persevere in trusting in the Father, even through death, makes death meaningful. In the end, it is not death that is tragic but our protecting ourselves against it. The message of Christ's death revealed in his resurrection is that our death is fulfillment. In the light of his death into resurrection, and in the promise of our own, it is now possible despite the chaos of it all to make a good choice for life. It would now be possible with that faith to eliminate all destructive weapons, renounce greed and exploitation and begin, even on earth, to build the kingdom of peace, justice and love. But society replies that it will never accept vulnerability, that it loves this life on which it is closed in and that it will continue to protect itself. To take Christ seriously, to love the enemy, is something it cannot afford to do. It is sad because they shall all die anyway. So it is up to the individual to choose a full life unfearful of others because in death there is nothing to lose. Death is not loss, but fulfillment.

This takes the "sting" and "victory" out of death, as St. Paul sees it. But it still continues to be the last enemy. It is always possible that for a selfish man it will be the final confirmation of his self-isolation, the "outer darkness" of Scripture. Paul says that it is in Christ that we must die. Paul is crucified with Jesus so that Jesus may live in him (Gal. 2:20; 6:14). Christ died and came to life to rule over the living and the dead (Rom. 14:9). The Christian experiences Christ's victory over death by sharing Jesus' death (Rom. 6:4). He died on behalf of all so that all might live, not for themselves but for him who died on their behalf (1 Cor. 5:14).

Since Christ has destroyed the destructive power of death and set us free, it is possible now to cherish beauty, goodness, loving others, the sacred and the holy. Old age is more than the end of productivity. It is a time to reap a rich harvest of wisdom, insight, contemplation, love and excitement for the future. This is the heritage in danger of being lost in our technological society, the heritage that death brings to full ripeness.

We have an instinct for life. We know instinctively that we are made for life, and that it is perfectly natural to wish to live forever. Death, therefore, is a physical (not a moral) evil. And so, because of the offer of life and fulfillment in our faith, it is normal and quite legitimate to want to resist death and rebel against it with our whole mind and body. If it is to be accepted at all, it must be for some transcendent motive. There is no value in accepting death for the wrong reasons—"half in love with easeful death," the easy way out, the cowardly refusal of life. But it is possible to accept it for positive reasons, to go trustingly into the mystery, to have faith in the future and to commend one's person to God. We have to take a look at how this chaotic event happens and what it implies.

Animals perish. We die. It is not merely our bodies that die. It is the whole person who dies. This is truly fearsome since we cannot just promise ourselves survival as disembodied spirits (a Greek idea). A disembodied spirit is not a human person; neither is a corpse. The whole person dies and therefore it takes God to bring that person through death to life. Only God can grant resurrection. We cannot achieve it through human endeavors. In other words, we do not survive death because we are good people, but because God is powerful to save. Death, then, calls for faith and a trusting surrender to God. The human person is a unity, not a combination of two separable entities—a separable soul imprisoned in a body. We are one. We are our spirit-enlivened bodies. For that reason the salvation preached by Paul (1 Cor. 15:36ff) is not the liberation of the spirit from the body, but the transformation of the whole person into a spiritualized body fashioned into the likeness of the glorified body of Christ (Phil. 3:21). "He will transfigure these wretched bodies of ours into copies of his glorious body." This new body ("body" meaning the whole person in Scripture) will no longer be the opaque body burdened by sinful flesh—the body that limits the person within time and space, making relationships fearful, memory untrustworthy, thought painful and the whole person vulnerable to what is without and within. The spirit will embody a spiritualized body transfigured in the Spirit of Christ, wholly free of all limitations.

This whole thing is beyond our capacity to understand because it is a mystery. However, a mystery is not something closed but something open to unending exploration. We have to try to explore this body question. We are all very well aware that we are more than neat, orderly robots. We are a mystery even to ourselves. We are more than can be seen. It is much too large for us because, in effect, we are the totality of our lived experience. We are, bodily, all that we have embodied into ourselves over the years. We are all that we have incorporated (corpus: body) through our relationships: childhood, parents, school, studies, colors, flowers, music, love, travel, history, struggles, faith and so much more. We have embodied it all, not merely an embodiment of a hundred and fifty pounds of meat and bone. We are today the product or the embodiment of all we have experienced through our relationships to people and things. It is as body that we establish the relationships through which we become who we are. As humans we are made for relationships. It is their variety and chaotic complexity that make us the unique personalities we are. Without relationships we would all be clones from the same mold. Our body is the web of relationships we have embodied as we lived our life. Who I am, the unified body-person who wishes to survive death, is the person I have become by embodying into myself all that I have related to in my experience of life. And in relating to another person I relate to the entire embodiment of that other person, so that in the end there is a vast web or net of relationships which is all people and yet is myself and is the body of Christ. Confused? Well, as I said, it is a mystery, but a magnificent one. One has to see it. It hardly bears explanation. However it is this embodiment of our total environment that provides the continuity of the body of flesh in this world with the spiritualized body in the next. We embody, not by grasping but by surrendering to all, letting all have a home in us. What dies is this whole embodied person and what rises is that same embodied person but now wholly set free and without the limitations of time and space and ignorance.

Brought to life in resurrection, within the body of Christ, it should be clear that the person's reward for a good life in the flesh will not be something distinct from the lived experience. Money given to a youth who mows the lawn has no relationship explicitly to the work itself. Our reward will not be something that has no relationship to the life we lived, but it will be the fullness of that life revealed in all its goodness. It will be divinized by the presence of God in it and transfigured by Christ. The reward for life will be that life itself, the entire embodiment given to us as our inheritance. The reward shall be the transfigured task we accomplish today as we give ourselves in a gift of love to others. Where there is no love there is no embodiment. Where there is love the whole body of Christ becomes our embodiment also. The reward, besides being our own unique body accomplished person, will in its fullness be also the whole body of Christ.

Dying, Christ brought his body—vine and branches, temple of living stones, head and members—his entire embodiment, into God's presence, thus creating heaven. He brought earth into God and his glory. And now, all of us who through an unselfish desire for life, through word and sacrament, are incorporated into him will die and rise with him. Death need have no fear for the person who loves. The risen person will be our very selves in our total bodies, the continuity of the fullness of who we are, the spiritualized rather than resuscitated body. No moment, no smallest experience, will be lost. And just as our body on earth was for relationships, so will our heavenly body be, but with all the limitations removed. We shall be presence and openness to all others. The instinct for life in greater abundance will be overwhelmingly fulfilled.

In the meantime, trust your chaos, even if you cannot yet celebrate it.